Rags to Rugs

Hooked and Handsewn Rugs of Pennsylvania

Schiffer® Publishing Ltd
4880 Lower Valley Road Atglen, Pennsylvania 19310

Patricia T. Herr

Other Schiffer Books on Related Subjects
Rug Hooking In Maine, 1838-1940, Mildred Cole Peladeau
The Big Book of Hooked Rugs, 1950-1980s. Jessie A. Turbayne
Modern Hooked Rugs. Linda Rae Coughlin
Hooked Rugs Today. Amy Oxford
How To Hook Rugs. Christine J. Brault

Library of Congress Control Number: 2008932959

Covers and book designed by: Bruce Waters
Type set in Kuenstler-heading font/New Baskervlle-text font

ISBN: 978- 0-7643-3125-1
Printed in China

Published by Schiffer Publishing Ltd.
4880 Lower Valley Road
Atglen, PA 19310
Phone: (610) 593-1777; Fax: (610) 593-2002
E-mail: Info@schifferbooks.com

In Europe, Schiffer books are distributed by
Bushwood Books
6 Marksbury Ave.
Kew Gardens
Surrey TW9 4JF England
Phone: 44 (0) 20 8392-8585; Fax: 44 (0) 20 8392-9876
E-mail: info@bushwoodbooks.co.uk
Website: www.bushwoodbooks.co.uk
Free postage in the U.K., Europe; air mail at cost.

Contents

Acknowledgments

In the spring of 2004, a season when all good things begin to sprout and grow, a dedicated group of rug hooking enthusiasts, teachers, and designers in the Lancaster Pennsylvania area had an idea. They were convinced it was the appropriate time to gather information on the antique rugs of the region and contemporary rug makers before some of this information was lost forever. We are indebted to these amazing people, and perhaps wondering why on earth we ever listened to, Peggy Hannum and the Honorable Leslie Gorbey. Thank you both for your hard work and guidance.

When presented with the idea, the staff of the Heritage Center Museum of Lancaster County: Peter Seibert, President; Kim Fortney, Vice President and Head of Education; Wendell Zercher, Curator; Sandy Ream, Office Manager; Leigh Mackow, Quilt Museum Site Manager; Erika Belen, Marketing Director; James Bollinger, School Programs Director; and Helene Tingle, former Marketing Director, saw this as an important opportunity to collect and preserve a part of southeastern Pennsylvania culture that has long been overlooked. As a result, a project patterned after the successful Lancaster County Quilt Harvest, or quilt documentation done by the Museum in the 1980s, was proposed.

This Rug Harvest took place during the years 2004 through 2006. With the help of museum volunteers and members of rug hooking guilds and interested and supportive people from Pennsylvania, Maryland, and New Jersey, this project became a reality. Thank you to these many hard working people: Ellen Albright, Carol Ambrozy, Patricia Baker, Liana Bauerle, Jean Bednarski, Cheryl Boyd, Joyce Brennen, Doloris Brown, Rebecca Buckwalter, Bill Byers, Judy Carter, Claudia Casebolt, Wendy Christie, Joyce Combs, France Couillard, Rebecca Erb, Lucia Ferrero, Cyndi Fisher, Ann Garee, Joan Garner, Barb Garrett, Karl Gimber, Mary Jo Gimber, Leslie Gorbey, Lisa Gress, Kris Haley-Paul, Henry Paul, Peggy Hannum, Bob Hannum, Dawn Heefner, Faye Hegener, Merle Heitmueller, Clarke Hess, Betty Hill, Roberta Horvath, Cindy Irwin, Tracy Jamar, Dolores Janns, Peg Kauffman, Carol Keefe, Alan Keyser, Sharon Kollman, Mary Kowal, Mary Margaret Kuhn, Sidney Kuhn, Dolores Little, Char Lough, Helen Lynch, Roberta Machalek, Laura Marshall, Mary Lynne Naples, Sharron Nelson, Don Nelson, Karen Novakoski, Sue Obetz, Marilyn Oehler, Martha Petkosh, Kathryn Potts, Kim Potts, Sally Raub, Janet Reid, Polly Reinhart, Lee Ridgway, Marion Sachs, Lucy Sanders, Ellen Savage, Yahna Schoenberger, Joyce

Figure 1. Gallery view of "Rags to Rugs: Pennsylvania Hooked and Handsewn Rugs" on exhibit at Heritage Center Museum of Lancaster's Quilt and Textile Museum, Lancaster, Pennsylvania November 17, 2007 through December 31, 2008.

Schroeder, Suzanne Seyler, Roberta Smith, Susan Stier, Marie Stotler, Wendy Sweigart, Phyllis Thompson, Georgia Townsend, Deb Tshudy, Elizabeth Volmer, Lina Warfield, Betsy Weidler, Margaret Wenger, Deborah Whitcraft, Suzanne White, and Dee Zimmerman.

Rugs of the southeastern region of the Commonwealth of Pennsylvania were carefully photographed and documented. Both antique rugs and those being created by contemporary makers were included, to help preserve and record these functional household objects before their stories and that of their makers were forgotten.

With this portion of the project completed, the museum staff, working closely with Judge Leslie Gorbey and the author, mounted the exhibition *Rags to Rugs: Pennsylvania Hooked and Handsewn Rugs* in the newly renovated and expanded Heritage Center Museum of Lancaster County Quilt and Textile Museum. Views of selected areas of the exhibit space are seen in Figures 1 through 5. To our knowledge, this is the first comprehensive collection of southeastern Pennsylvania hooked and handsewn rugs to be on public view.

We appreciate the lenders whose rugs were used in the exhibit and are illustrated in this book for their generous support and cooperation. Thank you to Bill Buckwalter, Judy Carter, Edwina Cholmeley-Jones, Gail Donahue, Roger and Marj Gerhart, Leslie Gorbey, Peggy Hannum, Ruth E. Heisey, Cindy Irwin, William and Barbara Hazlett, Clarke Hess, Landis Valley Museum, Judith Lile-Hynes, Anne Bedics and Thomas Kort, George Lyster, Carol A. Maxwell, Sam and Kathy McClearen, Michael McCue and Michael Rothstein, Ruth Hershey McGowan, Kathryn Moyer, Linda and Dennis Moyer, Sarah Muench, Nailor Antiques, Dr. Sharron V. Nelson, Jack and Ruth Nolt, Lena Nolt, Olde Hope Antiques, Lelia F. Ridgway, Mr. and Mrs. Irwin Schorsch, Evelyn Schreiber, Joane Smith, Steve Smoot Antiques, Margaret Wenger, Robert and Carolyn Wenger, and many unnamed Friends of the Heritage Center.

Long-time and new friends were helpful in sharing their ideas and research for this study. They include Jennie C. Baker; Linda Eaton, Winterthur Museum and Country Estate; Clarke Hess; Edwin Hild, Olde Hope Antiques; Donna Horst, Landis Valley Museum; Evelyn Lawrence; Michael R. Lear, Archives and Special Collections Assistant, Shadek-Fackenthal Library, Franklin & Marshall College; Tom Martin, Interpreter, Landis Valley Museum; Amelia Peck, The Metropolitan Museum of Art; and John Blanda and Shelly Wiles, Lebanon County Historical Society. A special thank you goes to Don Nelson for his photographic expertise that made the book's illustrations possible.

Figure 2. A portion of "Rags to Rugs" exhibit examining roll of personal expression in making of rugs.

Figure 3. Exhibit area in "Rags to Rugs" highlighting contemporary rug juried exhibit. This changing exhibit focused on rugs made by Pennsylvania artists and was divided into three four-month hangings: Animals, Flowers and Fruits, and Pictorials.

Figure 4. View of area featuring various communities of rug makers including Dauphin County cross-stitched examples.

Figure 5. Partial view of areas displaying Lancaster Amish rugs to left and figural and scenic examples to right.

The exhibit, *Rags to Rugs: Pennsylvania Hooked and Handsewn Rugs*, and publication of this book have been generously funded by The Coby Foundation, Ltd., New York. As a result of this support and the assistance of the aforementioned individuals, we have had the exceptional opportunity to document this amazing group of textiles, to publicly exhibit them, and to preserve a record of the project for others to read and appreciate.

Coby

Recognition for those supporting and influencing this project would not be complete if the name of Maude Zane (1924-1984) of Gap, Pennsylvania, were not mentioned. Maude ignited that spark of interest I had in rug hooking and collecting when I first became acquainted with her as an antiques dealer, collector, and teacher of rug hooking at the Landis Valley Museum in the early 1970s. Figure 6 is a snapshot of Maude demonstrating rug hooking at Landis Valley, and Figure 7 is the rug she was creating in that photo; it is the only rug made by Maude that remains in that museum's collection. Thank you Maudie!

Figure 6. Maude Zane (1924-1984) demonstrating rug hooking at Landis Valley Museum Craft Days, 1983, an annual event held at the Landis Valley Museum, Lancaster, Pennsylvania. *Photograph by Jennie C. Baker.*

Figure 7. Hen hooked rug, attributed to Maude Zane (1924-1984) c. 1983, example Maude was hooking as seen in previous photograph. Woven wool strips on burlap, cotton twill tape binding, 20" x 17.5". *Collection of Landis Valley Museum, Pennsylvania Historical & Museum Commission.*

Introduction

Hand hooked and sewn rugs found in southeastern Pennsylvania have many things in common with rugs from other parts of North America. Although important examples of early 19th c. hand sewn and hooked rugs have been found in New England, the majority of rugs documented in this area were made in the later 19th and 20th centuries.

As we discovered during the Heritage Center Museum's Rug Harvest, there were also some interesting variations of known techniques and forms, and some rug techniques and designs that appear to be unique to this region.

The method of hooking rugs in Pennsylvania is similar to that found in other areas of the United States and has been well described in many fine books published previously on this subject. A more detailed description of this process and examples of materials used in the creation of some of these regional rugs may be found in Chapter 1, "Making a Hooked Rug."

Another large group of floor and table coverings was constructed using an eyed needle instead of a hook. This group includes a number of techniques ranging from cross-stitching on burlap to appliquéing felt cutout pieces to a foundation fabric, along with an assortment of other interesting construction techniques that are all described in Chapter 2, "From the Eye of the Needle."

Because of limitations with the Heritage Center Museum Rug Harvest documentation project, we did not examine loom-woven carpeting or braided or crocheted rugs unless the techniques were incorporated within the hooked or handsewn pieces.

Although we documented many wonderful rugs made by contemporary artists of the region, in this book we examine and discuss only those objects, hooked or handsewn, that were produced by artisans and crafts people of the past.

The majority of rugs appear to have had use as normal household floor and table coverings. Unlike handmade quilts and coverlets of the period, few seem to have been stored away in unused condition in cupboards and blanket chests. Perhaps, as a result, when they became worn they were thrown away, increasing the relative rarity of eighteenth and early nineteenth century hand made rugs in southeastern Pennsylvania.

In examining the many objects included in this study, it was sometimes difficult to determine if a piece was made "just for nice," as the Pennsylvania German expression states, or if it were truly a salvage art based on necessity. In many cases it was probably a combination of both factors. However, we were fortunate to have excellent family histories and documentation on some examples. Time is running short to still be able to recover some of this information first-hand. It is important in all areas of the country to document artifacts before their stories are lost.

CHAPTER 1

Making A Hooked Rug

Because there are many instruction books available on the subject of rug hooking, it seems appropriate to only briefly discuss the subject as it specifically pertains to rugs found in this southeastern region of Pennsylvania.

A detail view of the front and back of a rug hooked from strips of woven wool material is pictured in Figure 8. The entire rug may be seen in Figure 129 on page 108. Fabric strips were frequently wool, but could have been mixtures of cotton, rayon, silk, and other blends of woven and knit textiles that were available. Figure 9 includes all of these fabrics in the hooking materials. This rug appears in Figure 109 on page 90. These examples might be considered make-do or salvage objects, but sometimes the maker used various materials for their artistic effect. The foundation through which the fabric strips or yarns were hooked or looped was most frequently burlap and sometimes bound with another fabric or twill tape. This is visible in the detail view.

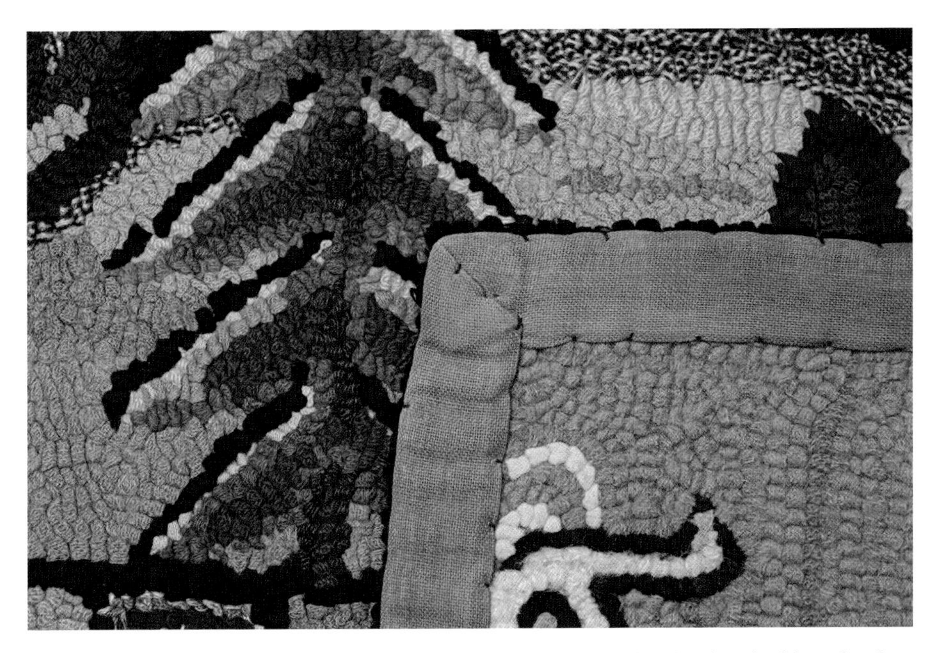

Figure 8. Detail of scenic rug, c. 1940, showing woven wool strips hooked into burlap foundation, bound with plain weave cotton tape, 32' x 53". See Figure 129 for overall image of rug. *Collection of Sam and Kathy McClearen.*

Figure 9. Detail of abstract patterned rug, c. 1940, containing blend of woven and knitted wool, and rag strips hooked into burlap foundation, bound with twill cotton tape. See Figure 109 for an overall image of the rug. *Collection of Kathryn Moyer.*

The strips could have been cut by hand, but machines like the Fraser cloth cutting device, seen in Figure 10, made this work easier, faster, and the strips more uniform. Harry Fraser, a rug hooker, designed this machine in 1948 as a clamp-on table top device. By changing the cutter blade, a rug hooker could cut strips ranging from 3/32 to 1/2 inch wide. This particular machine was purchased by Hilda "Sue" Beyer Landis in the 1950s.

In the late 1940s, while her husband was working, Landis took courses from a well known rug hooker and instructor, Vera Bisbee Underhill from nearby Millersville, Pennsylvania. An interview with Landis and numerous articles from local newspapers covering rug hooking activities, indicate that she and a group of other women in Lancaster County met on a regular basis at the home of Vera Underhill, not only to learn the craft but enjoy the company of other women.

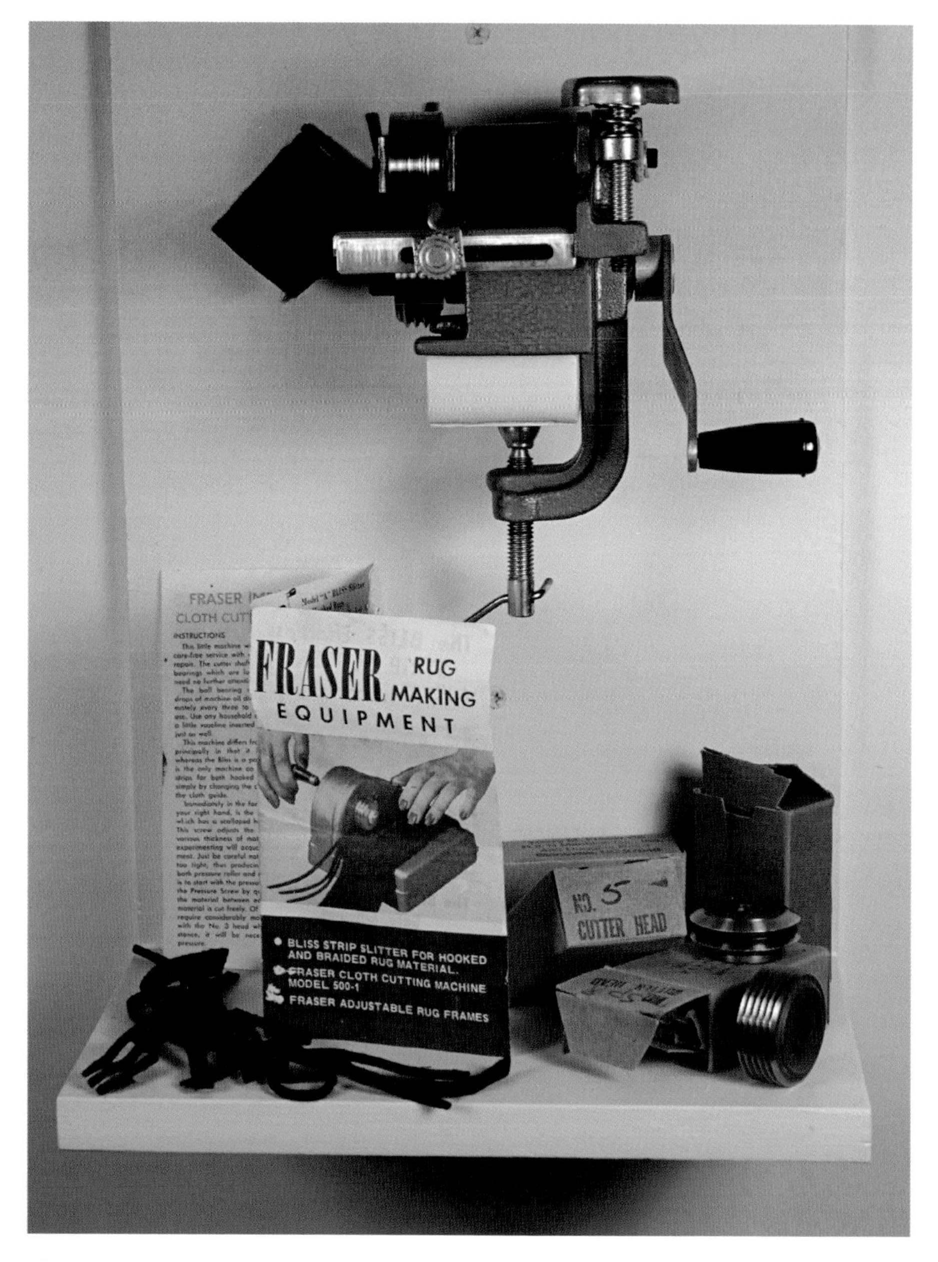

Figure 10. Fraser cloth cutting machine, cutter head, and brochures, c. 1950, purchased by Hilda "Sue" Beyer Landis in early 1950s to make her first rug. *Collection of Leslie Gorbey.*

Her unfinished rug, still on its original frame accompanied by her bucket of cut fabrics, is shown in Figure 11. Most rugs of any size were hooked on some type of similar rug frame. This was Landis' first and only rug project. The pattern of the unfinished rug was created by Caroline Saunders, who produced many of the patterns for Pearl McGown, a nationally known instructor, distributor, and creator of rug hooking patterns.

Figure 11. Unfinished hooked rug in frame and bucket of rug materials, c. 1952, owned by Hilda "Sue" Beyer Landis who began this, her first rug, in early 1950s. *Collection of Leslie Gorbey.*

Instead of cut strips of woven or knitted material some rug makers used yarns as their hooking material. Usually they were substantial plied wool or cotton yarns adding substance and thickness to make a serviceable rug. Figure 12 is a close up view of a rug attributed to Anna Denlinger Landis Charles of Lancaster. She made it in the image of a feed bag using an actual printed burlap bag as foundation material. The heavy wool yarns create a thick even layer on the surface of the rug. A photograph of the complete rug can be seen in Figure 161 on page 141.

Occasionally cotton was used instead of burlap for the foundation fabric. The button-eyed kitten mat, seen in Figures 37 and 38 on page 34, has a central hooked area done on a cotton foundation. Later rugs and most contemporary examples use a cotton canvas made for this purpose. Figures 106 and 107 on page 88 show a rug whose backing is made from a piece of cotton hand knit just for that purpose.

Figure 12. Detail of wool yarn hooking on burlap, c. 1979. See Figure 161, on page 141, an for overall view of the rug. *Collection of Robert and Carolyn Wenger.*

Figure 13. Five rug hooks attributed to Samuel S. Fair, Ephrata, Lancaster County, c. 1930. Last two hooks on right are ball hook (commercially made) and proddy tool (hand made), c. 2000. *Collections of Gail Donahue, Carol A. Maxwell, and Leslie Gorbey.*

Rug hooks varied from the earliest examples that were hand made through those that are commercially produced. Examples of 20th century handmade hooks attributed to Samuel S. Fair of Ephrata, Pennsylvania are seen in Figure 13 along with a commercially manufactured ball-handled hook and proddy tool on the far right.

There were many published sources of rug hooking, dying instructions, and patterns. The color swatches and book cover shown in Figure 14 were produced by Pearl McGown, of Massachusetts, in the 1950s. She was a well known figure in the world of rug hooking. Patterns were available through newspapers, periodicals, and companies catering to the popular craft of rug hooking.

Women created their own patterns, shared them with community and friends, as was the case with the Amish rugs seen in Figures 72 to 84 on pages 57 to 69. Women in the business of rug hooking, like Alice Potter Fordney, sometimes designed their own rugs, as illustrated by some of the small hand drawn and colored drawings of rug patterns found in her estate and illustrated in Figures 68 and 69 on page 54.

Figure 14. Color swatches and book cover produced by Pearl McGown, Massachusetts, c. 1955. *Collection of Cindy Irwin.*

CHAPTER 2

From The Eye Of The Needle

One of the earliest examples of needleworked rugs documented for this project is the rooster rug pictured in Figure 15.[1] It was worked with wool yarn using the satin stitch on a plain weave linen foundation. The technique, materials, and pattern are similar to designs worked on American pictorial needlework of the 18th century. The unknown maker probably drew her own pattern of confrontal roosters surrounded by floral motifs from some other textile or printed work that she had seen. She likely worked this piece on a frame similar to those used in making a needlework picture using coarse wool yarn instead of the fine silk thread used by a sampler maker. The edges of this rug appear wavy because the circular motifs of the needlework flowers have pulled the plain weave foundation out of alignment. A similar rug has been found using the same needlework technique and materials and features pairs of rampant lions and sheep.[2]

Figure 15. Rooster rug, unknown maker working in Pennsylvania, c. 1860. Satin stitched wool yarn on plain weave linen foundation, 33" x 44". *Private collection.*

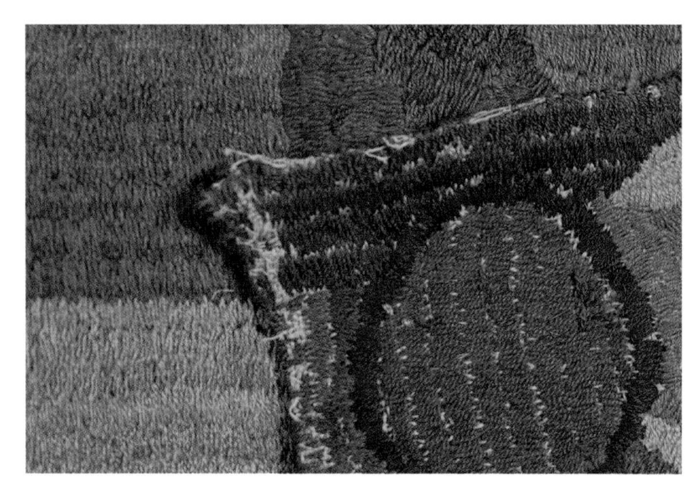

Figure 15a. Detail of rooster rug seen in Figure 15 showing both top and under surface. *Private collection.*

Elaborate figural appliquéd rugs that depict varieties of plants, animals, and other motifs have occasionally been found in southeastern Pennsylvania. These needle worked floor and table coverings and the more common appliquéd penny rugs were part of the later 19th century Victorian influence on home decorating. The rug illustrated in Figure 16, bearing the dates 1887 and 1899, is an example of how elaborate these appliquéd works can be. This fanciful piece is made up of colored felt fabrics appliquéd and decorative stitching added to create a complex needleworked design. Multicolor tongue or shoe heel-shaped felt pieces have been applied to create a decorative border.

Figure 16. Appliqued and needleworked rug, unknown maker working in Pennsylvania, dated 1887 and 1899. Wool felted and plain weave fabric appliquéd to twill weave cotton foundation, buttonhole and cross stitch decorated edges with felt tongue-shaped flaps, 27.5" x 46". *Collection of Landis Valley Museum, Pennsylvania Historical & Museum Commission.*

Another figural appliquéd rug attributed to Clara Hoffmanster of the Oley Valley in Berks County is seen in Figure 17. Although it is less colorful than the previous example it derives its bold effect from the realistic dark felt birds and animals appliquéd in a balanced design to a lighter cotton foundation. This example was probably made about 1900.

Figure 17. Appliqued and needleworked rug, attributed to Clara Hoffmanster, Oley Valley, Berks County. c.1900. Wool and cotton fabrics on linen foundation, with buttonhole, chain, cross, and outline stitch decoration, 28.5" x 46.5". *Photograph courtesy of Olde Hope Antiques.*

Figure 18. Detail of appliquéd and needleworked table rug seen in Figure 19 showing intricate combinations of appliquéd layers and wool needlework that produced this decorative cover. *Collection of Linda and Dennis Moyer.*

The rug shown in Figures 18 and 19 contains a variety of floral motifs that are appliquéd to a dark cotton foundation. Rather than being simple felt or woven wool flaps they are needleworked fabric layers that are given added color and height with wool yarn that is buttonhole, satin, and flat stitch; shirred; clipped; and plush work. Even the edge is scalloped and finished with contrasting colored yarn buttonhole stitching. This rug was found in Lehigh County and likely was made for table use and not for the floor.

Figure 19. Appliqued and needleworked table rug, unknown maker, Lehigh County, c. 1890. Wool yarn buttonhole, satin, and flat stitch: shirred; clipped; and plush work on plain weave cotton foundation with scalloped edges, 23.5" x 40". *Collection of Linda and Dennis Moyer.*

Another needleworked rug displaying the Victorian love for color and embellishment is seen in Figures 20 and 21. Merino yarns frequently used in Berlin work of the period decorate the burlap foundation with colorful and fanciful floral patterned stitching. Such fine needlework and materials hardly seems appropriate to serve as a floor covering and may have been used to decorate a table in a parlor or sitting room.

Figure 20. Detail of rug seen in Figure 21 showing needlework stitches used to cover burlap foundation. *Collection of Linda and Dennis Moyer.*

Figure 21. Floral needleworked rug, unknown maker, southeastern Pennsylvania, c. 1890. Merino wool yarn, satin, chenille, and sculpted stitches on burlap foundation, 33" x 59". *Collection of Linda and Dennis Moyer.*

"Over the top" in the needlework rug category is the only way to describe the fabric sculptural rug illustrated in Figure 22. Judging by its decorative motifs it was made to go over the top of a table to simulate a dinner setting. It is thought to have been made by a Schwenkfelder needleworker in the Montgomery County area of Pennsylvania.

The Schwenkfelders are a close knit religious group who emigrated to southeastern Pennsylvania from Silesia in Eastern Europe through Saxony to gain religious freedom. They have a long-standing Germanic needlework tradition, but this table rug can only be described as high Victorian in nature. It consists of multiple layers of now somewhat faded purple, pink, green, yellow and red fabric sculpture. Obviously not a functional tablecloth, one suspects it would have been classified by its Pennsylvania German maker as "just for nice."

Figure 22. Table rug, unknown Schwenkfelder maker, Montgomery County area, southeastern Pennsylvania c. 1890. Wool and metallic yarns, satin, buttonhole, shirred and sculpted stitches on wool foundation, machine made cotton lace edge, 32" diameter. *Collection of the Schwenkfelder Library & Heritage Center.*

During this same period in the late nineteenth century Log Cabin quilts were in vogue along with fancy needlework. However the example shown in Figure 24 is the only rug resembling a quilt that was documented during this Rug Harvest project. Constructed like a quilt this example is sized as a rug, and unlike a bedcovering, fringed on all sides. The top surface is made from wool fabrics which would also make it more practical as a table and not a floor covering. Figure 23 is a detailed view of one section of this handsome Straight Furrow pattern.

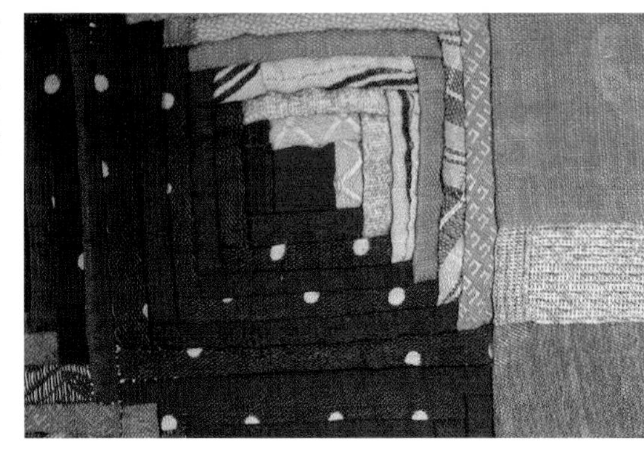

Figure 23. Detail of the Log Cabin rug, pictured in Figure 24, showing log cabin construction and variety of wool fabrics. *Collection of Linda and Dennis Moyer.*

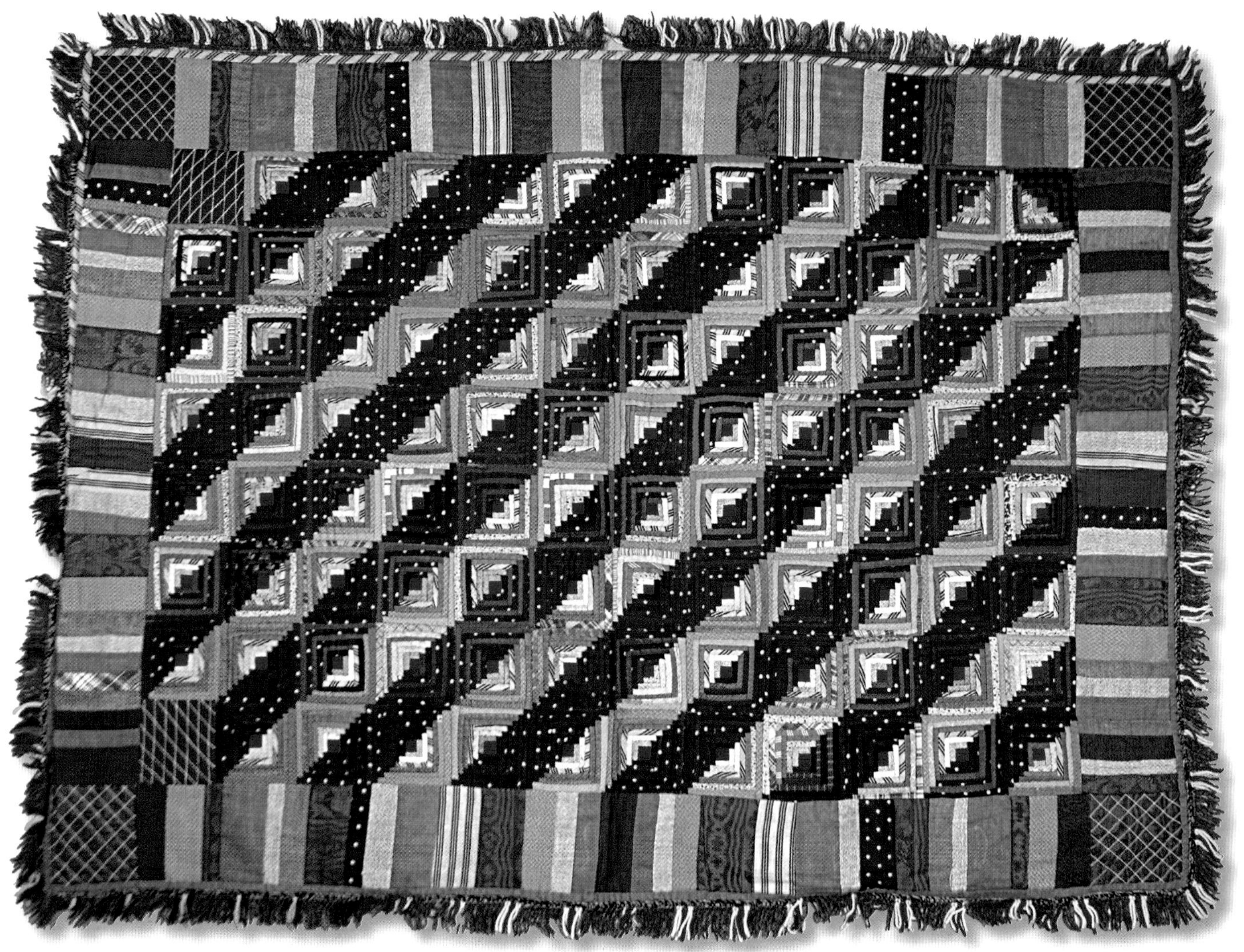

Figure 24. Log Cabin pieced rug, unknown maker, upper Montgomery or Lehigh County, c. 1875. Hand pieced wool fabrics, diamond pattern machine quilting, cotton twill weave fabric back, applied hand made wool fringe, 33" x 45". *Collection of Linda and Dennis Moyer.*

The more familiar and traditional appliquéd felt rugs seen throughout the United States in this late 19th and early 20th century period are commonly known as penny rugs. The hexagonal shaped example, pictured in Figure 26 with a detail shown in Figure 25, was probably used as a table rug, possibly under a lamp. Found in southeastern Pennsylvania it consists of layers of color-coordinated wool concentric circles sewn to a dark cotton foundation and edged with fine buttonhole stitching. The stitching was not only decorative but stabilized the cut edges of the fabric.

Another needlework technique used in Pennsylvania, as well as many other locations in the United States, is the Berlin patterned cross stitch design. These distinctive German patterns were used to create samplers, wall hangings, rugs, clothing, and any other surface in the Victorian home that could possibly have been decorated. Originally imported in the mid 19th c. as colored graph-like patterns with accompanying bright colored worsted wool matching yarns, the form spread throughout the country over the later part of the 19th c. The genre frequently featured romanticized animals and children and was heavily embellished with floral motifs.

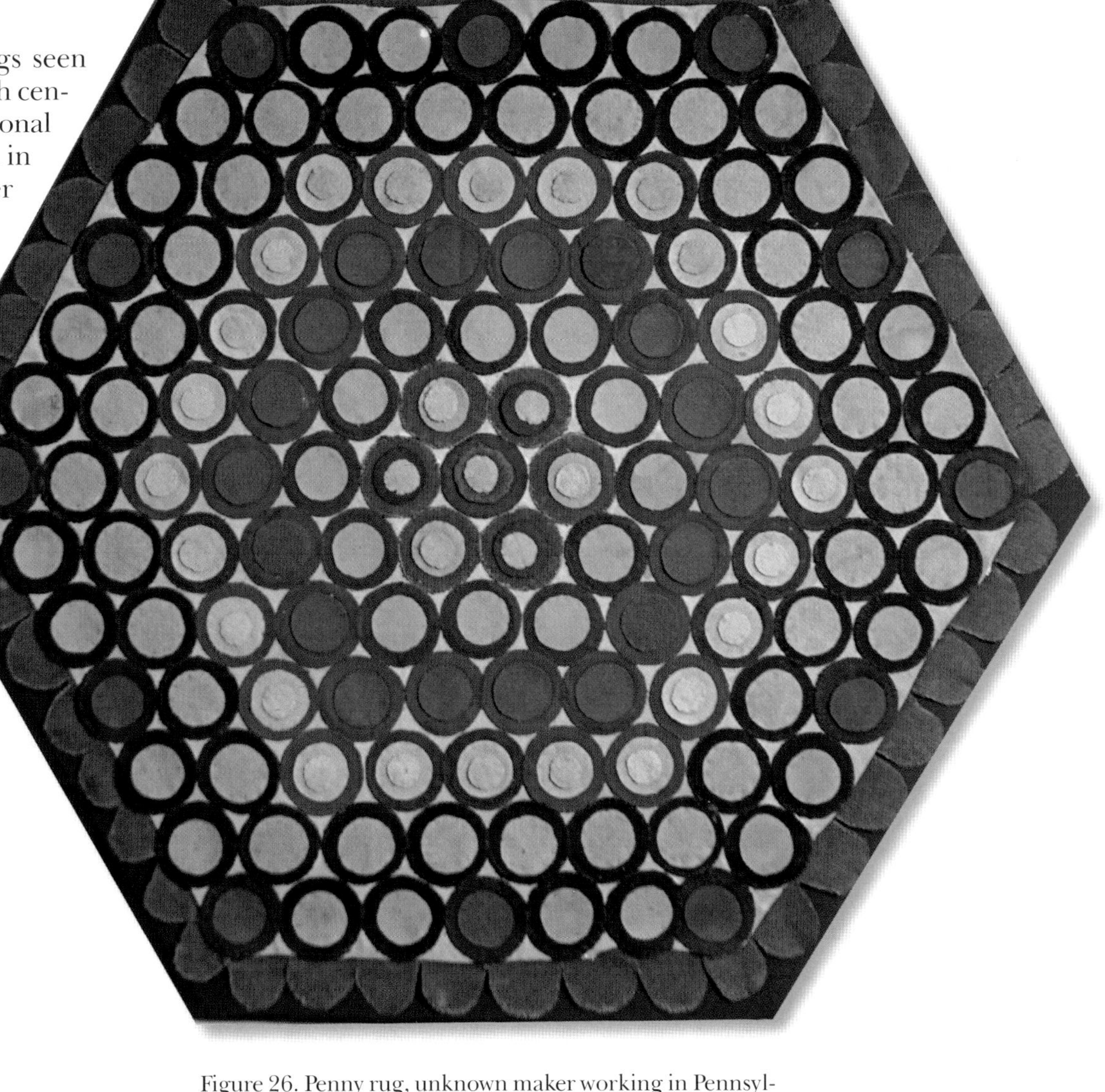

Figure 26. Penny rug, unknown maker working in Pennsylvania, c. 1890. Wool fabrics appliquéd on cotton foundation, cotton buttonhole stitch, applied cotton/wool blend scalloped edges, 32" x 37". *Collection of Judith Lile-Hynes.*

Figure 25. Detail of penny rug illustrated in Figure 26 shows finely worked buttonhole stitch finish on each "penny." *Collection of Judith Lile-Hynes.*

The rug in Figure 27 contains a spaniel-type dog, the date 1883 and the initials "M.S.," probably those of the maker. The elaborate form and shading of the initials and the leaf and vine border design is typical of Berlin work as is the applied crocheted fringe.

Figure 27. Berlin work spaniel rug, signed and dated "M. S./1883," unknown maker working in Pennsylvania. Wool cross stitch on burlap foundation, applied crocheted wool yarn fringe, 26" x 38". *Collection of Landis Valley Museum, Pennsylvania Historical & Museum Commission.*

A similar style of rug, from the same time period, is seen in Figure 28. It is attributed to one or both sisters: Maria L. (1866-1942) and Lizzie L. Hershey (1867-1953) born to Anna Landis Hershey and Samuel Hershey, whose home was in the Strasburg area of Lancaster County. These Mennonite women never married but lived together in the city of Lancaster where they worked as domestics. A photograph of the makers taken with a group of friends on the home farm is seen in Figure 29.

Their work features a dog sitting beside a young girl surrounded by a rose and leaf border. This pattern is more complex than the previous example because of the complexity of shading worked through the figures and flowers on their solid bright red background.

Figure 29. Photograph of Hershey girls and friends taken on home farm near Strasburg, Lancaster County, c.1886. Makers of rug seen in previous illustration (Figure 28), Maria and Lizzie Hershey, are standing first and second in front row on left side. *Collection of Bill Buckwalter.*

Figure 28. Berlin work girl and dog rug attributed to Maria L. (1866-1942) and Lizzie L. Hershey (1867-1953), Strasburg, Lancaster County, c. 1890. Wool cross stitch on burlap, cotton and wool plain weave back, applied commercially woven wool fringe, 27" x 44.5". *Collection of Bill Buckwalter.*

An example of cross stitching probably not influenced by the Berlin work pattern craze, but more a crossover from the Pennsylvania German coverlet pattern designs, is the southeastern Pennsylvania mat pictured in Figure 30. Fringed on three sides, this small piece was likely used as a table cover. It is signed and dated "Magdalene Snyder 1879," probably by the maker and the date it was finished. The patterns closely resemble those seen on woven Jacquard patterned coverlets. A coverlet with similar motifs is seen in Figure 31. It was woven by Jacob Andrews working in Manor Township, Lancaster County for a Mennonite client named Esther Habecker in 1835. Coverlets using similar patterns were made in many regions of Pennsylvania through the 1860s. It is likely that Magdalena copied her rug motifs from one of these old family bed-coverings. Another group of solidly cross-stitched rugs seen primarily in the Dauphin County area of Pennsylvania is discussed on page 76 and includes Figures 93 through 100.

Figure 30. Cross-stitched table rug signed and dated "Magdalene Snyder 1879." Rug was found in southeastern Pennsylvania. Wool cross-stitched on plain weave cotton foundation, tied yarn fringes on three sides, 15" x 26". *Private collection.*

Figure 31. Jacquard patterned coverlet woven by Jacob Andrews, Manor Township, Lancaster County for Esther Habecker, 1835. Rose, bird, and tree motifs similar to those on cross-stitched table rug seen in Figure 30. Wool and cotton, center seam, self-fringed, 100" x 85". *Collection of Clarke Hess.*

A small rug that may be related to the Dauphin County examples is illustrated in Figure 32. The maker Nora S. Stauffer was working about twenty-five years after most of the Dauphin County cross-stitched rugs were made. Although there are design differences between Nora's bold central star design and the smaller overall design seen in the Dauphin County pieces, the yarns and needlework techniques are similar. Nora, a Mennonite girl, lived only a few miles south of the Dauphin County makers in the Manheim area of northern Lancaster County. It is possible she had some social contact with the Lingle and Gingrich families and had seen their work.

Figure 32. Cross-stitched table rug signed and dated "1901 N. S. N.", attributed to Nora S. Stauffer, Manheim, Lancaster County. Wool cross-stitched on burlap, edges finished in wool buttonhole stitch, 19" x 37.5". *Collection of Clarke Hess.*

Rarely seen in Pennsylvania are rugs constructed from shirred fabrics that were applied to a foundation. Figure 33 is a small light weight rug that probably would have been impractical as a floor covering. In this example strips of cotton cloth were gathered, or shirred to make fluffy caterpillar-like lengths of cloth that were then hand sewn on to a burlap foundation. Figure 34 is a detail view of its construction. The anonymous maker of this piece used bold contrasting colors, worked in initials as the center motif, and surround this with colorful angular and linear borders.

Another type of needle worked rug, found most often in Lancaster County Amish made rugs is the pompon rug described and pictured on page 74, Figures 89 and 90. Other rug techniques such as the sculpted and clipped work found in New England were not seen during our rug documentation project.

Figure 34. Detail of shirred rug seen in Figure 33 showing long stitches on back (bottom side) of burlap foundation anchoring gathered, or shirred, strips of cotton to top surface. *Private collection.*

Figure 33. Shirred rug with initials "S.M.", unknown maker working in Pennsylvania. Cotton fabric strips sewn on burlap, 21" x 40". *Private collection.*

CHAPTER 3

Form and Function

There are not many records indicating what, if any, floor coverings were used in 18th c. farm and village homes in Pennsylvania. The most common form of rug that survives from the 19th and early 20th centuries is the flatwoven strip rag carpeting seen in Figure 35. This example was actually used in a Mennonite home in the so-called "best bedroom" of the Metzler family farmhouse located in the village of Sporting Hill, Rapho Township, Lancaster County. Jacob Metzler (1841-1906) and Elizabeth (Wenger) Metzler (1843-1929) would probably have purchased this strip carpeting from one of the many professional men weavers working in the area. Women of the household would cut up strips of recycled clothing materials (similar to those prepared for hooking), sew them together into long strips, roll them into large balls, and take them to the weaver. He would then use heavy cotton yarn as warp and produce long rolls of approximately 36-inch widths for household use. Lengths of carpet would then be cut, sewn together at the sides, and bound with tape at the ends to fit each room. Less commonly seen are the narrower strips of this same type of rag carpet made for use on stairways.

Figure 35. Rag carpet strip woven by unknown professional weaver working in northern Lancaster County, c. 1870. Removed from "best bedroom" of Jacob and Elizabeth Metzler home located in Sporting Hill, Rapho Township, Lancaster County. Cotton yarn warp and rag weft, 36" wide. *Collection of Clarke Hess.*

The flatwoven ingrain carpet pictured in Figure 36 was somewhat more expensive and probably used for the more formal public rooms in the home. This example was found in the parlor of a farmhouse belonging to Mennonites Joseph H. Gochnauer (1844-1930) and his wife Anna (Hostetter) Gochnauer (1849-1936). The house was located in Landisville, East Hempfield Township, Lancaster County. When they passed away their granddaughter Anna R. Gochnauer, who lived nearby, used it on her bedroom floor until about 1994. Ingrain carpeting, like rag carpet, was also made by professional weavers in yard-wide strips from commercially produced wool yarns and sewn together to accommodate each room.

Even with the wide availability of professionally made carpeting, women in 19th and early 20th century households created many types of rugs for multiple household purposes as well as floorcoverings. Among the more commonly seen forms are: welcome mats, table and lamp mats, and chair seats. Hooked stair carpets and pads were also made but none were available for documentation in this study. Research through the present time has not uncovered any southeastern Pennsylvania bed rugs.

In Chapter 5, the reader will see that there were some very specific classifications of rugs made by Lancaster Amish women. Note the example illustrated on page 71 in Figure 86 that is typical of the long narrow Shoe Heel rugs made to place in front of the sofa in the main social room in the home. Also, Amish designated other Shoe Heel rugs for specific use. The rug seen on page 72 in Figure 87 was used near an entryway to wipe one's feet.

Table rugs appear to have been used in southeastern Pennsylvania homes. They are less common than floor coverings. Fortunately these examples did not succumb to wear as a floor rug did explaining why a number of well-preserved examples have survived. The cross-stitched piece seen in Chapter 2, on page 28, Figure 30, signed and dated "Magdalene Snyder 1879," was likely made as a table cover.

Figure 36. Ingrain carpet strip woven by unknown professional weaver working in northern Lancaster County, c. 1870. Removed from parlor of Joseph and Anna Gochnauer farm located in Landisville, East Hempfield Township, Lancaster County. Wool yarn warp and weft, 36" wide. *Collection of Clarke Hess.*

Another small textile, only 10 1/2 inches square, is illustrated in Figures 37 and 38. It is constructed of hooked materials as well as appliquéd materials. Attributed to Mennonite Frances Buch Royer (1846-1925) of Earl Township, Lancaster County, it was likely made about 1890. The foundation material of this whimsical piece is made from blue and white checked cotton apron material. The central figure is a cat hooked into the checked material using variegated brown cotton rag and buttons for eyes. Red and brown wool circles, like those used in penny rugs, fill the background and the cat sits on a base of hand-crocheted cotton lace. All this is surrounded by a black wool felt border. The materials used appear to be scraps left over from other household sewing projects. Judging from the small size, uneven surface, and pictorial nature of this piece it may have been made as a wall decoration, or as the Pennsylvania Germans would say, "just for nice."

Figure 37. Detail of hooked and handsewn mat illustrated in Figure 38, showing corner including felt scalloped trim, appliquéd "pennies," applied lace, and hooked cat motif on checked cloth foundation. *Private collection.*

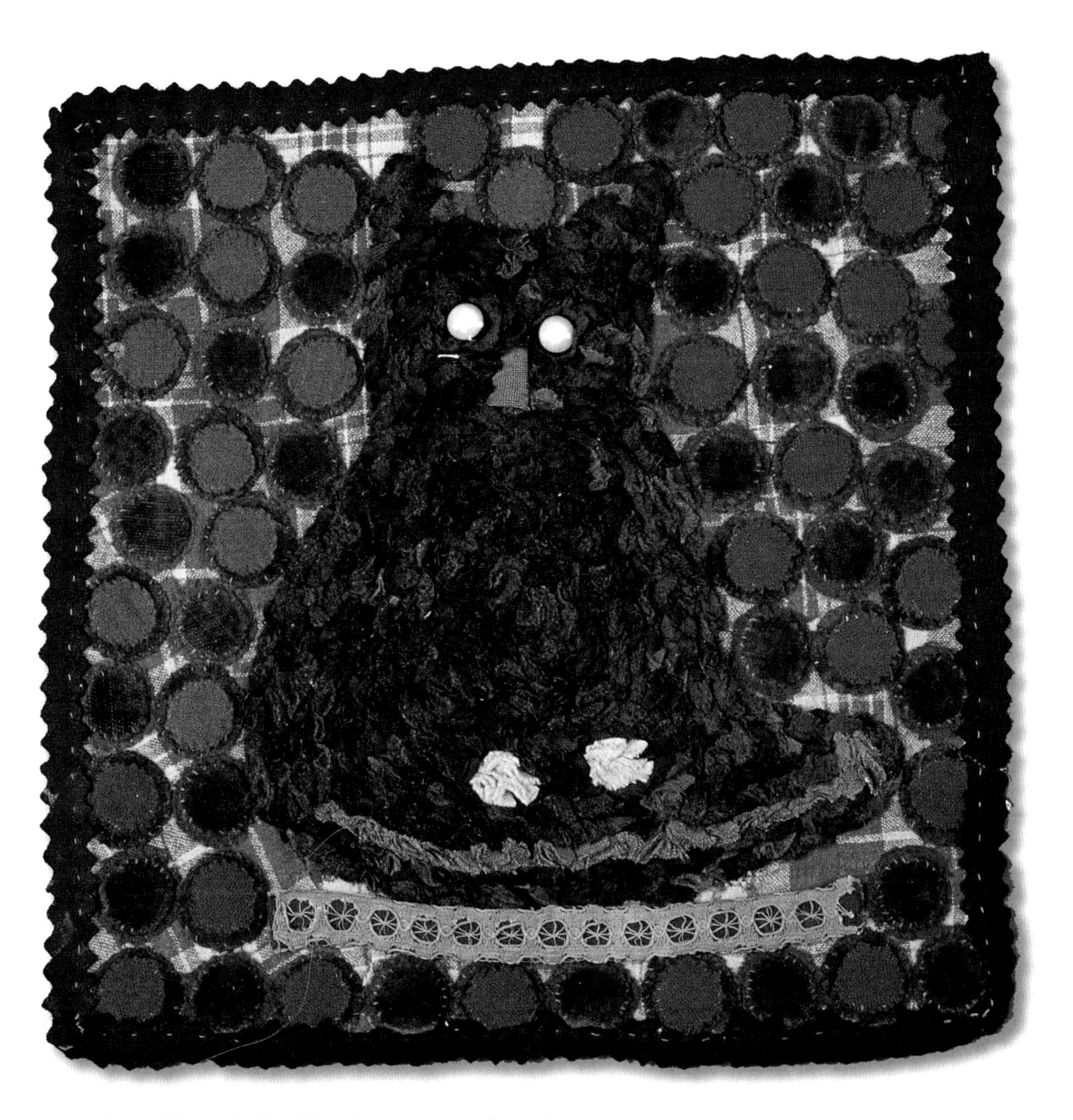

Figure 38. Hooked and handsewn mat attributed to Frances Buch Royer (1846-1925) East Earl Township, Lancaster County, c. 1890. Wool felt, buttons, cotton lace, and rag strips sewn and hooked to woven, blue check, cotton foundation, with applied wool felt edging, 10.5" square. *Private collection.*

Chair seats using a variety of decorative motifs were made either in sets or as individual creations. The majority of chair seats documented appear to have been made in the first half of the 20th century. The example shown in Figure 39 was probably made somewhat earlier in the late 19th or early 20th century. Its large size and shape suggest that it may have been used as a pad for a much earlier 18th century Chippendale chair.

Figure 39. Scroll motif D-shaped chair mat, unknown maker working in Montgomery County, c. 1900. Woven wool strips on burlap foundation, applied cotton backing, 13" x 17". *Collection of Linda and Dennis Moyer.*

It would be difficult to know, without a specific family history, if the small circular mat seen in Figure 40 was made as a chair or lamp mat. Its design certainly relates to some of the larger floor rugs picturing local landscapes such as the pieces shown in Chapter 9, on pages 106 to 109, Figures 127 to 130, all made in the 20th century.

Figure 40. House and barn motif chair mat, unknown maker working in southeastern Pennsylvania, c. 1940. Woven wool strips on burlap foundation, 13" diameter. *Collection of Linda and Dennis Moyer.*

The round floral patterned mat seen in Figure 41 appears to have been a chair seat. It came from a home in Lititz, Lancaster County and was probably made around 1960. It appears to have been from a commercial pattern and is hooked using cotton yarns. Such mats are still frequently found in area homes.

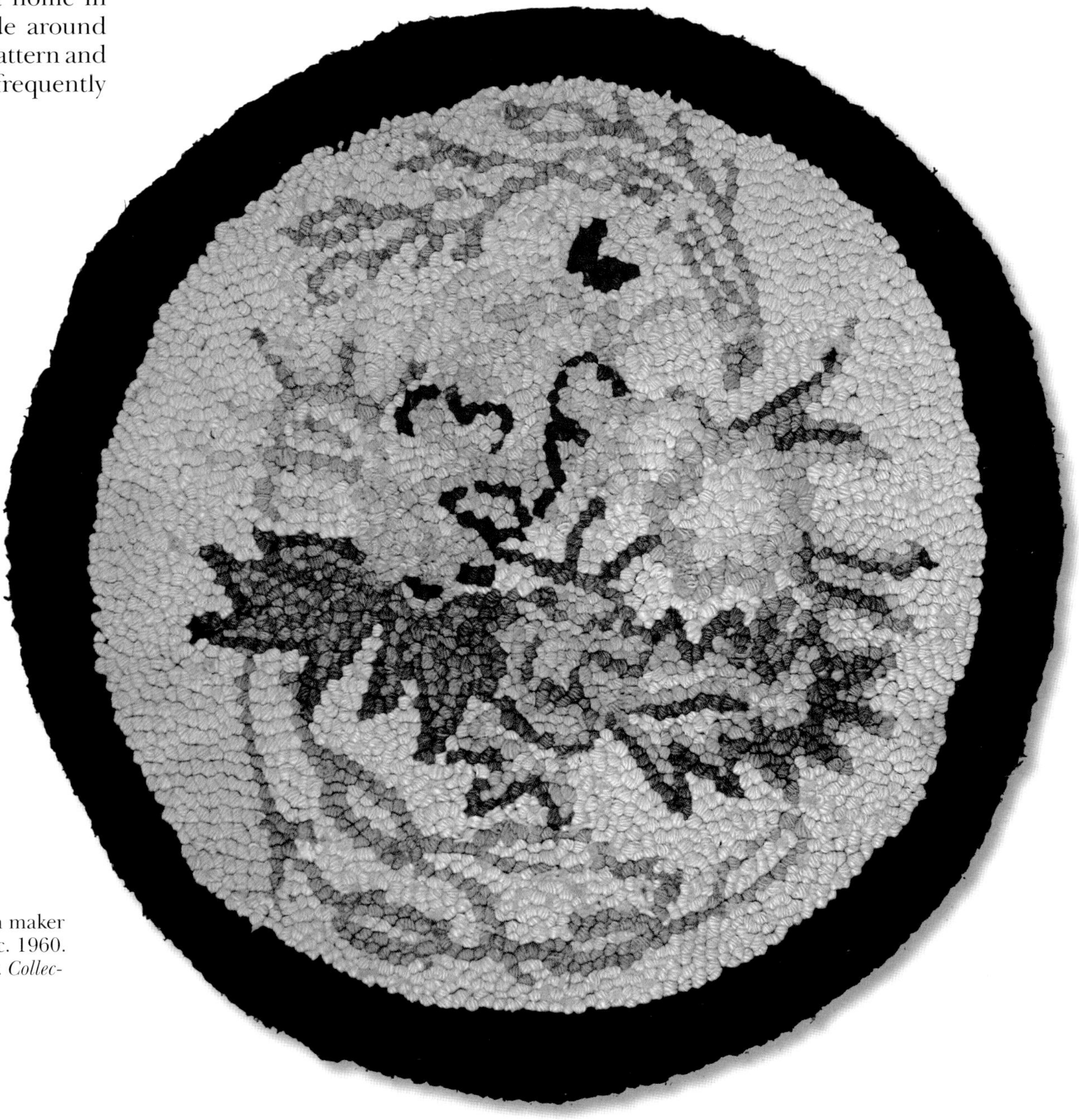

Figure 41. Floral chair mat, unknown maker working in Lititz, Lancaster County, c. 1960. Cotton yarn on burlap, 15" diameter. *Collection of Edwina Cholmeley-Jones.*

One of the most unusual chair seats, dating from about 1870, was found in Montgomery County and is pictured in Figures 42 and 43. It has a chain-stitched embroidered surface worked in fine Merino yarns. The foundation is probably a course cotton but it is completely covered by a printed cotton backing.

Figure 42. Detail of chair mat seen if Figure 43 showing fine merino wool chain stitched surface. *Collection of Linda and Dennis Moyer.*

Figure 43. Chain stitched floral chair mat, unknown maker working in Montgomery County, c. 1870. Merino wool yarn chain stitched on burlap foundation, cotton backing turned to front, 16" diameter. *Collection of Linda and Dennis Moyer.*

The buggy spread pictured in Figures 44 and 45 is not a rug but contains techniques used by rugmakers. Made by a member of the Old Order Mennonite Church in Lancaster County, this is a form still made and used by Amish and Old Order Mennonite residents. Both sects rely on horse drawn vehicles for personal transportation. This example is attributed to Emma Nolt of Eastern Lancaster County and was probably made about 1960. Emma was well known in her Old Order Mennonite community as a rug maker who used her own patterns to make hooked rugs and buggy spreads. She made this lap robe for her son Nemmo Nolt to use while traveling in his buggy. The flowers and leaves are hooked with yarn and embroidered with buttonhole stitching. Emma was known for making buggy spreads for members of her Old Order Mennonite Church when they purchased a new buggy.

The Pennsylvania Germans in particular seemed capable of creating decorative embellishments for all areas of the home and farm. So it is likely that future investigations and research will discover other interesting and useful forms of hooked and handsewn rugs.

Figure 45. Buggy spread, attributed to Emma Nolt, Old Order Mennonite woman working in Lancaster County, c. 1965. Wool yarn hooked and buttonhole embroidered on plain weave wool foundation, 47" x 41". *Collection of Lena Nolt.*

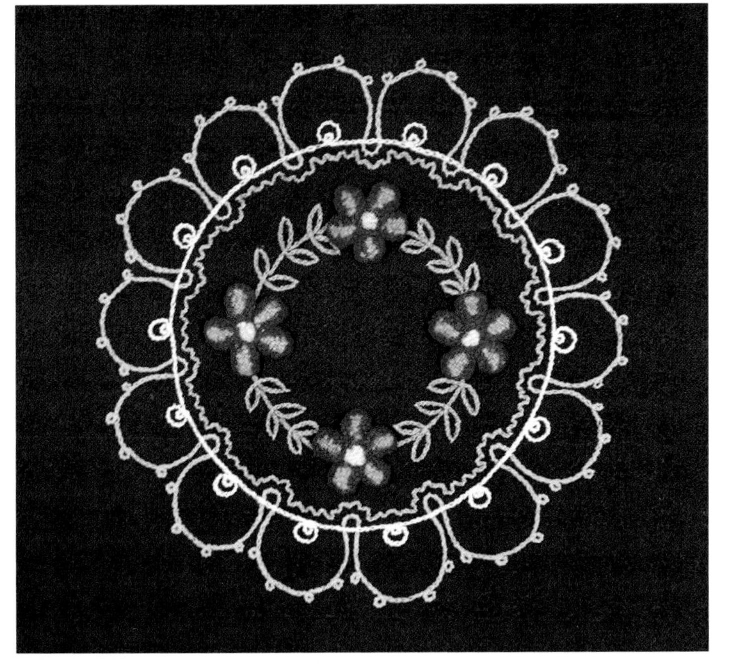

Figure 44. Detail of buggy spread illustrated in Figure 45 showing central area of lap robe embellished with yarn hooking and buttonhole stitching. *Collection of Lena Nolt.*

CHAPTER 4

The Business of Rugmaking

A number of rugmakers who made and sold their rugs for profit have been documented by the Heritage Center Museum's Rug Harvest. One example is Sallie Esh an Amish woman working in Lancaster County. An example of her work may be seen on page 52, Figures 65 and 66.

On a larger scale is the remarkable body of work produced by a business run by Alice Potter Fordney (1888-1973), daughter of Thomas Potter Fordney, Sr. and Ida Cox Fordney. Alice lived her entire life in Lancaster, Pennsylvania. Born into a socially prominent family, Alice spent her early years in the family home in the Rossmere section of the city attending private schools, participating in local social events, playing tennis, and traveling. The first mention of her sewing abilities is a notation in an irregularly kept diary written during the period between 1901 and 1905.[3] She lists 26 women for whom she had made collars. There is no mention if she charged a fee for these sewing projects.

There is evidence that she was an active dealer in antiques. Prior to this she spent some time as a dance instructor.[4] A few account books of her antiques business have survived from the years 1929-45. They list many small objects such as glass, silver, china, and a few pieces of furniture. Throughout the sales lists rugs appear that she sold to individual clients in prices ranging from $10-$30. A newspaper photograph and caption, seen in Figure 46, shows Alice participating in the first Lancaster Pennsylvania Antiques Show. She also exhibited at the first Wilmington Delaware show in the Hotel du Pont. Correspondence survives in the form of letters from Henry Francis du Pont, founder of Winterthur Museum in Delaware, concerning antique toys she had offered to him.

ANTIQUES displayed at the first Lancaster Antique show in the Brunswick displayed some of Lancaster's best traditions. Above Miss Alice Fordney shows three chairs from the old Grape Hotel one of Lancaster's more famous hostelries of yesterday, along with a number of other fine pieces.

Figure 46. Photograph of Alice Potter Fordney in her booth at first Lancaster Antiques Show held in 1935 at Brunswick Hotel in downtown Lancaster. Lancaster Sunday News, March 31, 1935, "*Camera Angles on the News,*" pg. 12. *Collection of theShadek-Fackenthal Library, Frankllin and Marshall College.*

Fordney also had an interesting relationship with Armstrong Cork Company, a leading manufacturer of linoleum flooring, whose headquarters is located in Lancaster, Pennsylvania. A letter seen in Figure 47, dated March 12, 1941 and written by Armstrong decorator Hazel Dell Brown, thanks Fordney for producing the "patriotic stair carpet" used in a full page color magazine advertisement. The image of the advertisement, seen in Figure 48, that accompanied Brown's letter, was published in issues of *Parent's Magazine* (March 1941), *Better Homes and Gardens* (March 1941), and *Good Housekeeping* (April, 1941).

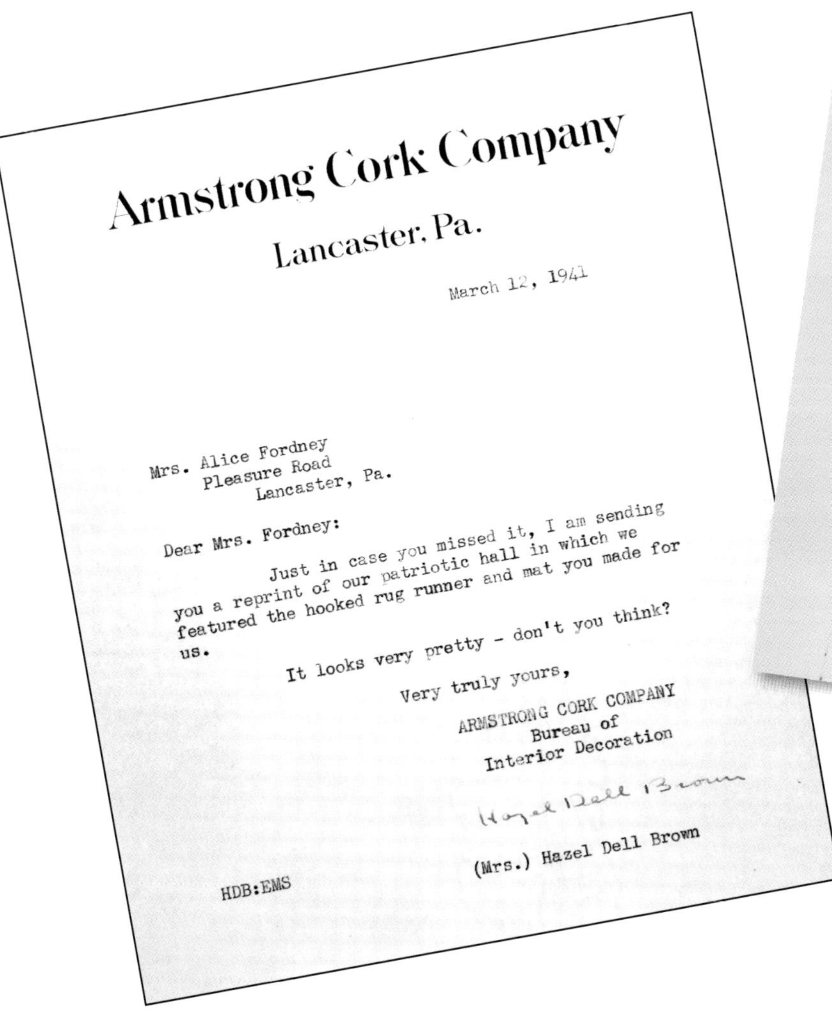

Armstrong Cork Company

Lancaster, Pa.

March 12, 1941

Mrs. Alice Fordney
Pleasure Road
Lancaster, Pa.

Dear Mrs. Fordney:

Just in case you missed it, I am sending you a reprint of our patriotic hall in which we featured the hooked rug runner and mat you made for us.

It looks very pretty - don't you think?

Very truly yours,

ARMSTRONG CORK COMPANY
Bureau of
Interior Decoration

Hazel Dell Brown

(Mrs.) Hazel Dell Brown

HDB:EMS

Figure 48. Image of advertisement mentioned in letter, seen in Figure 47, Fordey's stair carpet appears in left forground. *Collection of the Heritage Center Museum of Lancaster County.*

Figure 47. Letter from Armstrong Cork Company decorator, Hazel Dell Brown, thanking Alice Potter Fordney for producing the "patriotic stair carpet" seen in full page color magazine advertisement reproduced in Figure 48. 1941. *Collection of the Heritage Center Museum of Lancaster County.*

In one letter Higby provided Alice with names of local rug hookers he knew, living in small towns of Denver and Stevens in Lancaster County, whom she might hire if she had not already done so. Another letter asks when the rugs of "pattern #9121 covered wagon" would arrive as they have sold two of them. This may refer to the pattern used to create the rug exhibited in the foreground on the far right of a photograph, seen in Figure 49 taken of Fordney's booth at an unidentified antiques show.

Figure 49. Photograph of Alice Potter Fordney's booth at unnamed antiques show, c. 1935. Note large number of rugs on display, Conestoga wagon pattern rug at far right and floral runner in center aisle. *Collection of theShadek-Fackenthal Library, Frankliln and Marshall College.*

Figure 50. Paper pattern for portion of rug pictured in Figure 51, found along with the rug in the belongings of Alice Potter Fordney. *Collection of the Heritage Center Museum of Lancaster County.*

Also notice the rug on the floor in the center of Alice's booth, shown on page 42. It appears to be the same pattern, and possible the same rug as the rug and associated pattern hung in the 2008 "Rags to Rugs" exhibit at the Heritage Center Museum of Lancaster's Quilt and Textile Museum. Figures 50 and 51 show a pattern for a portion of the rug and the partially unrolled section of this long rug.

In a letter dated "March twenty-first 1944" Mr. Higby adds a P. S. asking, "Did you ever think of making your rugs out of a fine wool yarn?" Higby also asks for a discount on the price when buying large numbers and describes the company business in this paragraph.

"I have to mark these rugs so that they can be sold to the decorators who in turn have to mark them up and sell them to their clients, so you see there are many transactions before the rug is laid in the home. We only sell through the decorators and do not have a retail business."

Figure 51. View of partially unrolled runner that appears to be same pattern, possibly same rug, as runner on floor of Fordney's antiques booth photograph illustrated in Figure 49. *Collection of the Heritage Center Museum of Lancaster County.*

A letter dated 4-17-1945 from a Springfield, Massachusetts antiques dealer, Albert Steiger Company, lists a number of small antiques objects such as china, bottles, tin, several pieces of furniture and two rugs priced at $25 and $15. Eight letters from E. Higby of F. Schumacher & Co., New York City also survive. The company was ordering specific designs and forms such as "the fan design" and "the welcome rug." A rug and pattern similar to his description were found in the Muench family estate and are pictured in Figures 44 and 45.[5] He also suggests that they can send her canvas as some of their other suppliers use rather than the burlap Fordney was using at the time.

Figure 52. Pencil, ink, and watercolor design of rug pictured in Figure 53, attributed to Alice Potter Fordney, Lancaster, Pennsylvania, c. 1940. *Collection of the Heritage Center Museum of Lancaster County.*

Figure 53. Fan rug with loops for display, found in Alice Potter Fordney belongings, Lancaster Pennsylvania, 1940. Woven wool strips on burlap foundation, 23" x 36". *Collection of the Heritage Center Museum of Lancaster County.*

A photograph, shown in Figure 55, of a Pennsylvania German motif rug was also found in the Muench/Fordney papers. It appears to be the same pattern as the rug pictured in Figure 56. At least two examples of this rug have been found, differing only in the shade of the tan background. It is possible some of these examples were produced by Alice Fordney's shop. The design source for this pattern was obviously one of a pair of almost identical fraktur made for husband and wife, Peter and Catharina Guth, attributed to Christian Good (1779-1838), a Mennonite preacher in Lancaster County.[6] The example made for Catharina appeared in *Pennsylvania German Illuminated Manuscripts*, published by the Pennsylvania German Society of Norristown, Pennsylvania in 1937. This was the first illustrated book produced on Pennsylvania fraktur, was widely distributed in Southeastern Pennsylvania, and was likely the inspiration for this rug pattern. Peter's similar presentation piece is seen in Figure 57. Other Pennsylvania German motif rugs, seen in Figures 58 and 59 also belonged to Fordney. Designers of hooked rugs were not above "borrowing" from earlier folk art motifs.

Figure 55. Photograph of Pennsylvania German motif rug pattern found in Fordney's possessions, c. 1935. *Collection of the Heritage Center Museum of Lancaster County.*

Figure 56. Pennsylvania German motif rug, attributed to Alice Potter Fordney shop, c. 1935. Woven wool strips on burlap foundation, 39.5" x 87.5". *Collection of Olde Hope Antiques.*

Figure 57. Presentation fraktur made for Peter Guth (1800-1863), attributed to Christian Good, 1834. Ink and watercolor on wove paper, 10" x 8". *Collection of Mrs. Richard Flanders Smith.*

Figure 58. Semi-circular pomegranate in a pot rug, attributed to Alice Potter Forney's shop, c. 1935. Woven wool strips on burlap foundation, cotton twill tape binding, 22" x 34". *Collection of the Heritage Center Museum of Lancaster County.*

Figure 59. Semi-circular tulip in a pot rug, attributed to Alice Potter Forney's shop, c. 1935. Woven wool strips on burlap foundation, cotton twill tape binding, 25.5" x 37". *Collection of the Heritage Center Museum of Lancaster County.*

Evidence that Alice may have actually done rug hooking in her own home comes from a partially finished rug on a frame shown in Figure 60 that was among the objects in the estate of Alice's niece, Sarah Muench. Also part of the of this Muench collection are two rectangular rugs, pictured in Figures 61 and 62, bound and fitted on one side with hanging loops suggesting that they may have been used in a showroom, antiques show, or exhibit space.

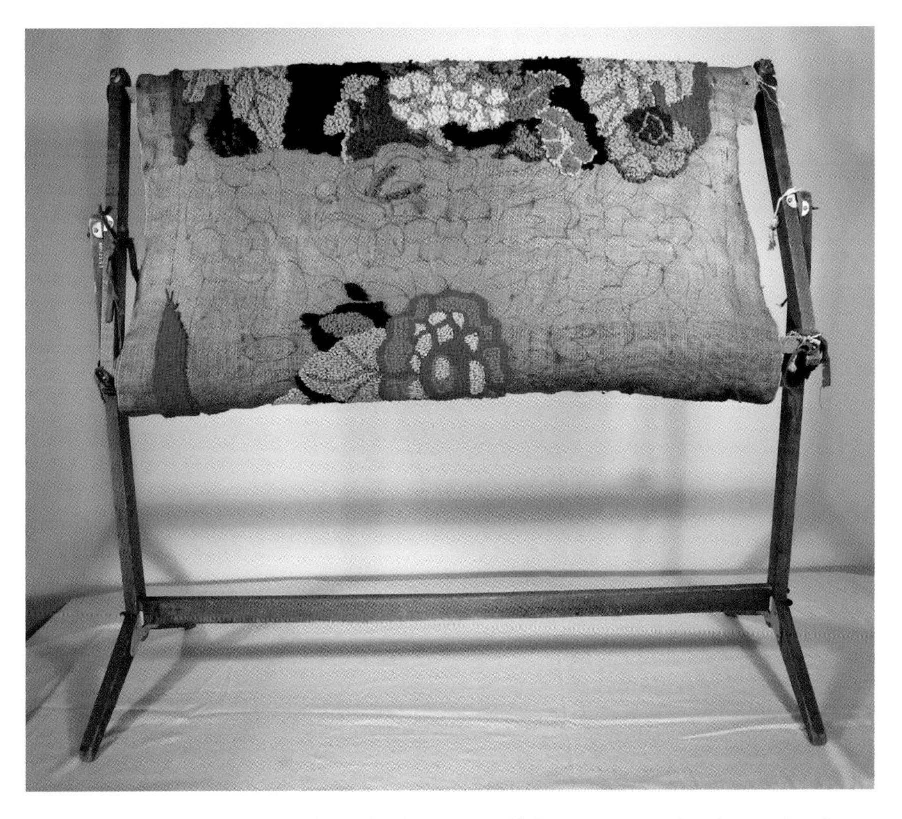

Figure 60. Unfinished floral rug in frame, c. 1970. Woven wool strips on burlap foundation, commercial wooden and metal frame.Rug attributed to Alice Potter Fordney (1888-1973), c. 1972. *Collection of the Heritage Center Museum of Lancaster County.*

Figure 61. Rooster rug with loops for display, found in Alice Potter Fordney belongings, Lancaster Pennsylvania, 1940. Woven wool strips on burlap foundation, 24" x 36". *Collection of the Heritage Center Museum of Lancaster County.*

Figure 62. Rocking horse rug with loops for display, found in Alice Potter Fordney belongings, Lancaster Pennsylvania, 1940. Woven wool strips on burlap foundation, 24" x 36". *Collection of the Heritage Center Museum of Lancaster County.*

A group of patterns and instruction sheets produced by the Priscilla Company. as seen in Figures 63 through 64, were apparently popular items in Fordney's business. The estate had multiple copies of these instruction sheets and several brown paper patterns for a rug picturing a central stylized flower basket and flanking birds. Although no completed rugs of this pattern were found in the Muench/Fordney belonging, two of these rugs are pictured in Figures 65 and 66. They were purchased in Mastersonville, Lancaster County and attributed to Ida Garman a resident of that village. They appear to have been made around 1940, during the same time period that Fordney was active. The color ways however are not the same as those suggested by the color codes on the brown paper patterns.

An interview with Sarah McIlvaine Muench,[7] Alice Potter Fordney's niece, reveals more personal details about Aunt Alice and her entrepreneurial hooked rug business. Sarah said:

"....she was a character. Warm and artistic. A business woman who ran an antiques business including a hooked rug business.... Aunt Alice did make some hooked rugs, but mostly she used Mennonites and other local country people whom she called her 'ruggers.' She provided the designs as well as the colors.... she was fussy about colors. She went around to local wool mills, finding the color fabrics she wanted."

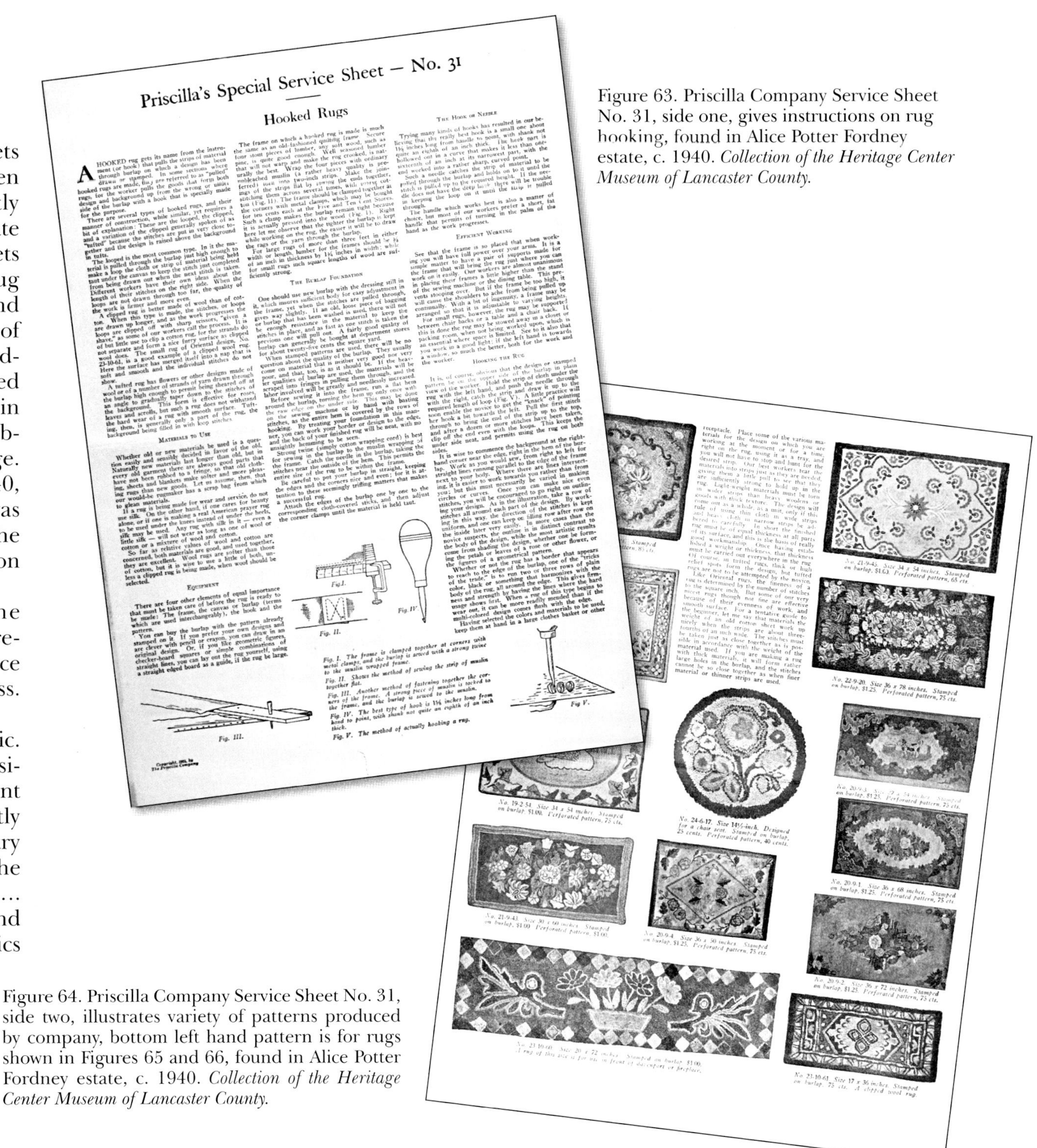

Priscilla's Special Service Sheet — No. 31

Hooked Rugs

A HOOKED rug gets its name from the instrument (or hook) that pulls the strips of material through burlap on which a design has been drawn or stamped. In some sections where hooked rugs are made, they are referred to as "pulled" rugs, for the worker pulls the goods that form both design and background up from the wrong or under side of the burlap with a hook that is specially made for the purpose.

There are several types of hooked rugs, and their manner of construction, while similar, yet requires a bit of explanation: These are the looped, the clipped, and a variation of the clipped generally spoken of as "tufted" because the stitches are put in very close together and the design is raised above the background in tufts.

The looped is the most common type. In it the material is pulled through the burlap just high enough to make a loop the cloth or strip of material being held taut under the canvas to keep the stitch just completed from being drawn out when the next stitch is taken. Different workers have their own ideas about the length of their stitches on the right side. When the loops are not drawn through too far, the quality of the work is firmer and more even.

A clipped rug is better made of wool than of cotton. When this type is made, the stitches, or loops are drawn up longer, and as the work progresses the loops are clipped off with sharp scissors, "given a shave," as some of our workers call the process. It is of but little use to clip a cotton rug, for the strands do not separate and form a nice furry surface as clipped wool does. The small rug of Oriental design, No. 23-10-61, is a good example of a clipped wool rug. Here the surface has merged itself into a nap that is soft and smooth and the individual stitches do not show.

A tufted rug has flowers or other designs made of wool or of a number of strands of yarn drawn through the burlap high enough to permit being sheared off at an angle to gradually taper down to the stitches of the background. This form is effective for roses, leaves and scrolls, but such a rug does not withstand the hard wear of a rug with smooth surface. Tufting, then, is generally only a part of the rug, the background being filled in with loop stitches.

Materials to Use

Whether old or new materials be used is a question easily and sensibly decided in favor of the old. Naturally new materials last longer than old, but in every old garment there are always good parts that have not been rubbed to a fringe, so that old clothing, sheets and blankets make softer and more pleasing rugs than new goods. Let us assume, then, that our would-be rugmaker has a scrap bag from which to glean materials.

If a rug is being made for wear and service, do not use silk. On the other hand, if one cares for beauty alone, or if one is making a real American prayer rug to be used under the knees instead of under the heels, silk may be used. Any rug with silk in it — even a little silk — will not wear as long as one of wool or cotton or a mixture of wool and cotton.

So far as relative values of wool and cotton are concerned, both materials are good, and used together, they are excellent. Wool rugs are softer than those of cotton, but it is wise to use a little of both, unless a clipped rug is being made, when wool should be selected.

Equipment

There are four other elements of equal importance that must be taken care of before the rug is ready to be made: The frame, the canvas or burlap (terms which are used interchangeably), the hook and the pattern.

You can buy the burlap with the pattern already stamped on it. If you prefer your own designs and are clever with pencil or crayon, you can draw in an original design. Or, if you like geometric figures, checker-board squares or simple combinations of straight lines, you can lay out the rug yourself, using a straight edged board as a guide, if the rug be large.

The frame on which a hooked rug is made is much the same as an old-fashioned quilting frame. Secure four stout pieces of lumber, any soft wood, such as pine, is quite good enough. Well seasoned lumber that will not warp and make the rug crooked, is naturally the best. Wrap the four pieces with ordinary unbleached muslin (a rather heavy quality is preferred) torn into two-inch strips. Make the joinings of the strips flat by sewing the ends together, stitching them across several times, with strong cotton (Fig. II). The frame should be clamped together at the corners with metal clamps, which may be bought for ten cents each at the Five and Ten Cent Stores. Such a clamp makes the burlap remain tight because it is actually pressed into the wood (Fig. I). Right here let me observe that the tighter the burlap is kept while working on the rug, the easier it will be to draw the rags or the yarn through the burlap.

For large rugs of more than three feet in either width or length, lumber for the frames should be ⅞ of an inch in thickness by 1¾ inches in width; while for small rugs inch square lengths of wood are sufficiently strong.

The Burlap Foundation

One should use new burlap with the dressing still in it, which insures sufficient body for easy adjustment in the frame, yet when the stitches are pulled through, gives way slightly. If an old, loose piece of bagging or burlap that has been washed is used, there will not be enough resistance in the material to keep the stitches in place, and as fast as one stitch is taken the previous one will pull out. A fairly good quality of burlap can generally be bought at department stores for about twenty-five cents the square yard.

When stamped patterns are used, there will be no question about the quality of the burlap. They usually come on material that is neither very good nor very poor, and that, too, is as it should be. If the heavier qualities of burlap are used, the materials will be scraped into fringes in pulling them through, and the labor involved will be greatly and needlessly increased.

Before sewing it into the frame, run a flat hem around the burlap, turning the hem up only once with the raw edge on the under side. This may be done on the sewing machine or by hand with basting stitches, as the entire hem is covered by the rows of hooking. By treating your foundation in this manner, you can work your border or design to the edge, and the back of your finished rug will be neat, with no unsightly hemming to be seen.

Strong twine (simply cotton wrapping cord) is best for sewing in the burlap to the muslin wrapping of the frame. Catch the needle in the burlap, taking the stitches near the outside of the hem. This permits the entire size of the rug to be within the frame.

Be careful to put your burlap in straight, keeping the edges and the corners nice and even; for it is attention to these seemingly trifling matters that makes a successful rug.

Attach the edges of the burlap one by one to the corresponding cloth-covered sticks, and then adjust the corner clamps until the material is held taut.

The Hook or Needle

Trying many kinds of hooks has resulted in our believing that the really best hook is a small one about 1½ inches long from handle to point, with shank not quite an eighth of an inch thick. The hook part is hollowed out in a curve that makes it less than one-sixteenth of an inch at its narrowest part, with the end worked into a rather sharp, curved point.

Such a needle catches the strip of material to be pulled through the burlap and holds on to it until the stitch is pulled up to the required height. If the needle does not have the deep hook there will be trouble in keeping the loop on it until the strip is pulled through.

The handle which works best is also a matter of choice, but most of our workers prefer a short, fat handle that permits of turning in the palm of the hand as the work progresses.

Efficient Working

See that the frame is so placed that when working you will have full power over your arms. It is a simple matter to have a pair of supports made for the frame that will bring the rug just where you can work on it easily. Our workers are almost unanimous in placing their frames a little higher than the stand of the sewing machine or the dining table. This prevents stooping over. But if the frame be too high, it will cause the shoulders to ache from being pulled up continually. With a bit of ingenuity, a frame may be arranged so that it is adjustable to varying heights.

For small rugs, however, the rug may be supported between chair backs or a table and a chair back. If this is done the rug may be stowed away in a closet or packing room, when not being worked upon, which is an essential where space is limited. See to it also that you work in a good light; if the left hand is towards a window, so much the better, both for the work and the worker.

Hooking the Rug

It is, of course, obvious that the design or stamped pattern be on the upper side of the burlap in plain view of the worker. Hold the strip of cloth under the rug with the left hand, and push the needle through with the right, catch the strip and draw it up to the required length of loop (Fig. V). A little practice will soon enable the novice to get the "knack" of pointing her hook a bit towards the left. Pull the first stitch through to bring the end of the strip up to the top, and after a dozen or more stitches have been taken, clip off the end even with the loops. This keeps the under side neat, and permits using the rug on both sides.

It is wise to commence the background at the right-hand corner near the edge, right in the hem of the burlap. Work as you would sew, from right to left for straight lines running parallel to the edge of the frame next to your body. Where there are lines intersecting, it is easier to work towards you rather than from you; but this must necessarily be varied in making circles or curves. Once you can make nice even stitches, you will be encouraged to go right on outlining your design. As in the illustration, take a row of stitches all around each part of the design. By working in this way, the direction of the stitches is kept uniform, and one can keep on filling row after row on the inside later very easily. In more cases than the novice suspects, the outline is in distinct contrast to the body of the design, while the most artistic results come from shading the design, whether one be forming the petals or leaves of a rose or other flower, or the figures of a geometrical pattern.

Whether or not the rug has a border that appears to reach to the edge of the burlap, one of the "tricks of the trade" is to run two or three rows of plain color, black or something that harmonizes with the body of the rug, all around the edge. This gives firmness and strength by having the lines where the hard usage shows first. When a rug of this type begins to wear out, it can be more readily mended than if the multi-colored design comes flush with the edge.

Having selected the colors and materials to be used, keep them at hand in a large clothes basket or other

Fig. I. The frame is clamped together at corners with metal clamps, and the burlap is sewed with a strong twine to the muslin wrapped frame.

Fig. II. Shows the method of sewing the strip of muslin together flat.

Fig. III. Another method of fastening together the corners of the frame. A strong piece of muslin is tacked to the frame, and the burlap is sewed to the muslin.

Fig. IV. The best type of hook is 1½ inches long from head to point, with shank not quite an eighth of an inch thick.

Fig. V. The method of actually hooking a rug.

Copyright, 19[illegible], by The Priscilla Company

No. 21-9-43. Size 34 x 54 inches. Stamped on burlap, $1.63. Perforated pattern, 65 cts.

No. 22-9-20. Size 36 x 78 inches. Stamped on burlap, $1.25. Perforated pattern, 75 cts.

No. 19-2-54. Size 34 x 54 inches. Stamped on burlap, $1.00. Perforated pattern, 75 cts.

No. 24-6-17. Size 14½-inch. Designed for a chair seat. Stamped on burlap, 25 cents. Perforated pattern, 40 cents.

No. 20-9-1. Size 36 x 68 inches. Stamped on burlap, $1.25. Perforated pattern, 75 cts.

No. 20-9-4. Size 36 x 36 inches. Stamped on burlap, $1.25. Perforated pattern, 75 cts.

No. 20-9-2. Size 36 x 72 inches. Stamped on burlap, $1.25. Perforated pattern, 75 cts.

No. 23-10-61. Size 17 x 36 inches. Stamped on burlap, 75 cts. A clipped wool rug

Figure 63. Priscilla Company Service Sheet No. 31, side one, gives instructions on rug hooking, found in Alice Potter Fordney estate, c. 1940. *Collection of the Heritage Center Museum of Lancaster County.*

Figure 64. Priscilla Company Service Sheet No. 31, side two, illustrates variety of patterns produced by company, bottom left hand pattern is for rugs shown in Figures 65 and 66, found in Alice Potter Fordney estate, c. 1940. *Collection of the Heritage Center Museum of Lancaster County.*

Figure 65. Flower pot and flanking birds rug, light brown background, attributed to Ida Garman, Mastersonville, Lancaster County, c. 1940. Woven wool strips on burlap foundation, 20" x 72". *Collection of Steve Smoot Antiques.*

Figure 66. Flower pot and flanking birds rug, dark brown background and other colorway varying from rug illustrated in Figure 65, attributed to Ida Garman, Mastersonville, Lancaster County, c. 1940. Woven wool strips on burlap foundation, 20" x 72". *Collection of Steve Smoot Antiques.*

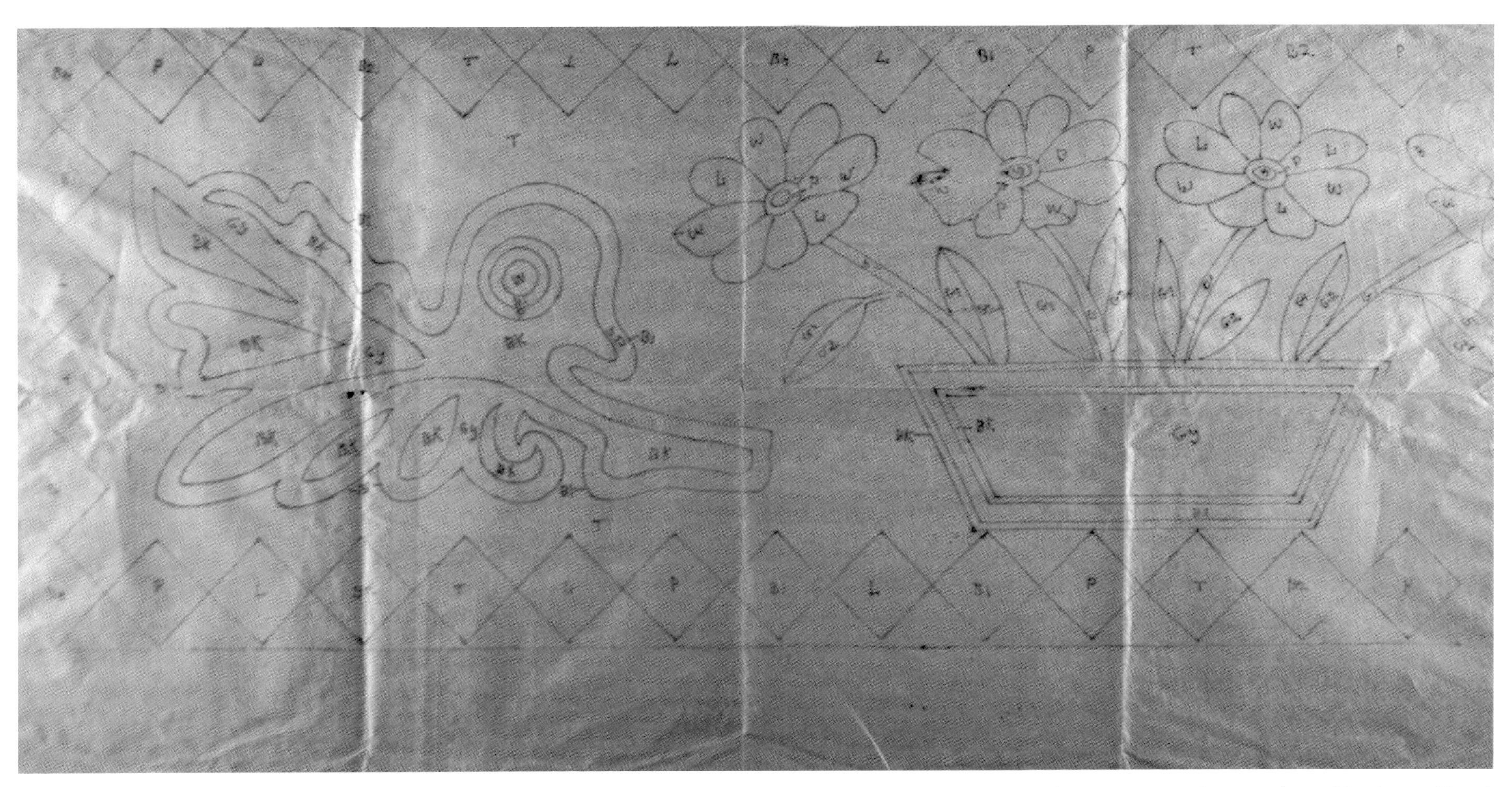

Figure 67. Paper pattern for rugs pictured in Figures 65 and 66, alphabetical abbreviations for color suggestions are lettered inside various areas of pattern, 24" x 47.5". *Collection of the Heritage Center Museum of Lancaster County.*

Figure 68. Ink and watercolor design for semicircular dog rug, attributed to Alice Potter Fordney (1888-1973), c 1940, 8" x 10". *Collection of the Heritage Center Museum of Lancaster County.*

Sarah Muench's comments concerning her aunt being "fussy about colors" is reinforced when seeing just two of the colorful hand drawn rug patterns, illustrated in Figures 68 and 69, amid the many notes, instructions, and other patterns found in the estate.

Figure 69. Ink and watercolor design for rectangular floral and scroll rug rug, attributed to Alice Potter Fordney (1888-1973), c 1940, 8" x 10". *Collection of the Heritage Center Museum of Lancaster County.*

Figure 70 pictures a section of the museum's exhibit "Rags to Rugs" that highlights some of the Alice Potter Fordney materials belonging to the Museum. The Heritage Center Museum of Lancaster County is privileged to have so many objects from the Sarah Muench collection to help tell the story of this commercial facet of rug making in southeastern Pennsylvania.

Figure 70. Introductory area of alcove in "Rags to Richs" exhibit, focusing on Alice Potter Fordney's commercial rug making business.

CHAPTER 5

Rug Making Within The Community

Community influences have shaped rug making in Pennsylvania for generations. People often came together to share techniques, patterns, and materials. Perhaps the best example of the influence of a community on rug production can be seen among the members of the close knit Lancaster County Old Order Amish settlement. Others, such as a group of rural Derry Township rugmakers, who shared access to a specific type woolen yarn--likely yarn remnants from a weaving mill--produced an amazing body of unusual cross-stitched rugs and mats.

Lancaster County Amish Rugs

Significant home production of hooked rugs by members of the Lancaster Amish community appears to have become popular in the mid-1930s. Prior to this period, and even today, the common floor covering found in Amish homes would have been strips of rag carpet sewn together to cover the majority of floor space within most rooms. This flatwoven rag carpet seen in Figure 71 was made by local Amish men who were professional weavers. Women cut their old clothing into think strips, sewed them together, and rolled the long pieces into balls for the weaver to use as filler or weft in weaving the carpet. The resulting floorcovering had a purple, blue, and green coloring that reflected the usual shades found in Amish clothing.

Diary annotations by Amish women writing in the mid-1930s and 40s refer to "ruggins" similar to quilting bees being held at regular intervals among neighboring families and friends. By the 1960s rug hooking as a social event appears to have fallen out of favor.[8] But rug making is still an important activity among members of the Amish community. Talented rugmakers, usually unmarried women, have become well known throughout southeastern Pennsylvania as rug makers selling their products and patterns as a means of support.[9]

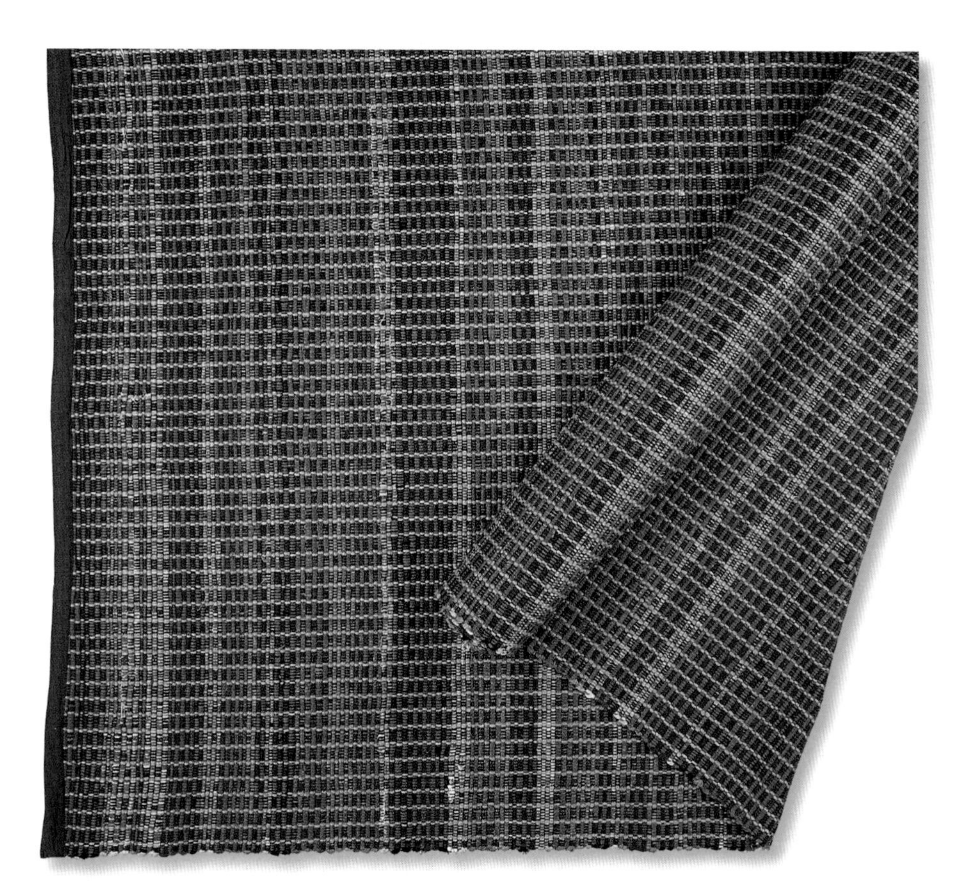

Figure 71. Rag carpet, unknown Amish professional weaver, Lancaster County, c. 1960. Wool and rag weft, cotton yarn warp, 36" wide. *Private collection.*

The streak of lightening rug illustrated in Figure 72 contains evenly cut and hooked wool and rag strips salvaged from family clothing. These familiar greens, pinks, reds, purples, blues, and yellows are the materials from which Lancaster Amish women made their family men's shirts and women's dresses. These are the colors also favored by the Amish in decorating other textiles, furniture, and household objects.

Figure 72. Streak of lightening rug, attributed to Mrs. Henry King, Gordonville, Leacock Township, Lancaster County, c. 1950. Woven wool and rag strips on burlap foundation. 20.5" x 43". *Collection of the Heritage Center of Lancaster County, given by George Lyster in memory of Kimberly Ann Bupp.*

Sallie Esh (?-1985), an unmarried Amish woman who lived in Intercourse, Lancaster County Pa. was well-known in the Amish community as a professional rug hooker. She also sold her products to the "English," a term the Amish use to designate non-Amish people. Her "Home Sweet Home" hooked rug, made in the 1940s, is seen in Figure 73. The pattern is similar to wall plaques made by Amish artists to hang in the home.

Figure 73. "Home Sweet Home" rug, attributed to Sallie Esh, Intercourse, Leacock Township, Lancaster County, c. 1945. Woven wool strips on burlap foundation, 24" x 40". *Collection of the Heritage Center of Lancaster County, given by George Lyster in memory of Kimberly Ann Bupp.*

Sallie's rug is typical of Lancaster Amish rugs. As the close-up view in Figure 74 reveals, the rug is hooked with evenly cut and precise rows of wool strips made from recycled Amish clothing. As a result most Lancaster Amish rugs contain the typical Amish color choices: black, blues, purples, turquoise, pinks, and greys. The central design motif, in this case the lettering, is surrounded by leaves, pansies, and roses; all frequently used Amish motifs. The foundation material used is plain weave burlap. Patterns such as this were made by, reused and passed among members of the local community.

Figure 74. Detail of "Home Sweet Home" rug seen in Figure 73, revealing evenly cut precise rows of all wool recycled Amish clothing fabrics. *Collection of the Heritage Center of Lancaster County, given by George Lyster in memory of Kimberly Ann Bupp.*

Examples of a rug and its matching pattern are pictured in Figures 75 and 76. Note the similarity to the previous examples in floral and leaf patterns and colors. This rug varies from the other Amish examples illustrated because it has a scalloped border and variegated brown background color. The maker, Fannie Stoltzfus, who lived near White Horse in Salisbury Township, Lancaster County, made the rug sometime between 1920 and 1940. Her pattern, typical of those used by Lancaster Amish hookers, is made of brown paper with punched holes delineating the pattern. The burlap foundation was then marked by pouncing or dusting blue chalk onto the brown paper so the dots of the pattern would be transferred as a guide for the rug hooker.

Figure 75. Floral rug, attributed to Fannie Stoltzfus, near White Horse, Salisbury Township, Lancaster County, c. 1930. Woven wool strips on burlap foundation, 31" x 44". *Collection of the Heritage Center of Lancaster County, given by George Lyster in memory of Kimberly Ann Bupp.*

Figure 76. Paper pattern for rug illustrated in Figure 75, c. 1930, attributed to Fannie Stoltzfus, near White Horse, Salisbury Township, Lancaster County, c. 1930. Holes in pattern are highlighted with blue chalk that was used to "pounce" or transfer pattern onto burlap foundation, 36" x 46". *Collection of the Heritage Center of Lancaster County, given by George Lyster in memory of Kimberly Ann Bupp.*

Figure 77. Pansy rug, attributed to member of Stoltzfus family, Intercourse, Leacock Township, Lancaster County, c. 1960. Wool yarn on burlap foundation, 16.25" x 27". *Collection of the Heritage Center of Lancaster County, given by George Lyster in memory of Kimberly Ann Bupp.*

The pansy rug shown in Figure 77 is smaller than most rugs found in the Amish community and unusual because it was hooked with yarns and not cut woven strips and contains a single predominant floral motif with no borders. The pansy is a favorite motif used in rugs, needlework and quilting patterns throughout the Lancaster Amish community.

Animal motif rugs were also popular with Amish makers. Horses, because they were such an integral part of the Amish culture appear in many variations on rugs. Figures 78, 79, and 80 are variations on this theme. Note that the pair of harnessed horses in Figure 78 appears to be trotting over the landscape without any attached buggy and share between them only six legs. The design for an almost identical rug attributed to Salome Stoltzfus is said to have been developed by her brother Aaron L. Smucker around 1930 and used primarily as a pattern for Amish boys' rugs.[10] This pattern with slight variations was popular among Amish rug makers working between 1930 and 1960. The pansies used in this example appear in many other Amish rugs.

Another interpretation of a team of horses is illustrated in Figure 79, but it still relies on a central cartouche with background fence and floral surround for its organization. The horse and buggy rug seen in Figure 80 is less geometric and seems to be an individual interpretation with a surrounding landscape and even a driver within the carriage. Representation of a human figure is rarely seen in Amish decorative arts.

Figure 78. Horse team rug, unknown Amish maker working in Lancaster County, c. 1940. Woven wool and rag strips on burlap foundation, 23" x 41". *Private collection.*

Figure 79. Horses in pasture rug, unknown Amish maker working in Lancaster County, c. 1940. Woven wool strips on burlap foundation, 22" x 43.5". *Collection of the Heritage Center of Lancaster County, given by George Lyster in memory of Kimberly Ann Bupp.*

Figure 80. Horse and buggy rug, unknown Amish maker working in Lancaster County, c. 1935. Woven wool strips on burlap foundation, 27" x 37". *Collection of the Heritage Center of Lancaster County, given by George Lyster in memory of Kimberly Ann Bupp.*

Other creatures were also depicted on Amish rugs. A popular design among Amish and English was that of a swan. The Amish popularized this rug using their own color schemes and regularly cut even rows of hooking. Figures 81 and 82 are two rugs made in the 1930s by unknown Amish hookers using a similar pattern with slight variations.

Figure 81. Swan rug, unknown Amish maker working in Lancaster County, c. 1935. Woven wool and rag strips on burlap foundation, 23" x 34". *Collection of the Heritage Center of Lancaster County, given by George Lyster in memory of Kimberly Ann Bupp.*

Figure 82. Swan rug, unknown Amish maker working in Lancaster County, c. 1935. Woven wool and rag strips on burlap foundation, 23" x 29.5". *Collection of the Heritage Center of Lancaster County, given by George Lyster in memory of Kimberly Ann Bupp.*

The bluebird rug, seen in Figure 83, is attributed to Linda Fisher. It combines birds as the central motif with surrounding geometric, scroll, and floral designs; all executed in the typical bright Amish hues. Dated rugs are less common, but the 1944 example, illustrated in Figure 84 incorporates simple outlined birds and the frequently seen pansies. It is possible it was made for a significant event such as a marriage or birth of a child.

Hooking was not the only method of rug making employed by Amish women. The appliquéd rug, the most common of which we know as the penny rug, is frequently seen in Amish homes. These appear to have been made during the same period as the Amish hooked rugs, beginning in the first quarter of the twentieth century. As with other textile production in the Amish community, there appears to have been a time lag from when this technique first became popular in the United States.

Figure 83. Bluebird rug, attributed to Linda Fisher, Witmer, East Lampeter Township, Lancaster County, c. 1945. Woven wool strips on burlap foundation, 26" x 42". *Collection of the Heritage Center of Lancaster County, given by George Lyster in memory of Kimberly Ann Bupp.*

Figure 84. Bird and pansy rug dated "1944," unknown Amish maker working in Lancaster County. Wool yarn and rag strips on burlap foundation, 22" x 37". *Collection of the Heritage Center of Lancaster County, given by George Lyster in memory of Kimberly Ann Bupp.*

The penny rug pictured in Figure 85 is similar to appliquéd rugs produced by non-Amish makers in the late nineteenth century and early twentieth century. In this example, made between 1920 and 1940, multicolored wool felt circles were sewn to a red cotton foundation and embellished with coordinating colored wool decorative stitching. The edges of this piece were finished in a typical Amish manner with a contrasting crocheted wool strip. The use of bright contrasting reds, pinks, greens, maroons, and black, often seen in Amish quilts and other needlework is also typical of Amish appliquéd rugs.

Figure 85. Penny rug, unknown Amish maker working in Lancaster County, c. 1930. Woven wool fabric and wool yarn appliquéd on cotton foundation, 34" x 58". *Collection of the Heritage Center of Lancaster County, given by George Lyster in memory of Kimberly Ann Bupp.*

More commonly seen in Amish homes are the appliquéd rugs referred to by the Amish as shoe heel rugs. Similar to the penny rug, the appliquéd wool fabrics are cut into flaps resembling the heel of a shoe. Like the penny rug, the free edges are outlined with contrasting wool yarn buttonhole stitching. The long narrow form of the shoe heel rug, seen in Figure 86, is often referred to by the Amish as a Sofa rug, as it was used in the best room in the house in front of the sofa. The "Welcome" rug, seen in Figure 87, was probably made for the floor of the spare bedroom or guest room, often referred to as the "dark room" by the Amish. When not in use the dark window shades, commonly seen in Amish homes, were kept down, making an ideal place for textile storage. Rugs and wall plaques saying "Welcome" and "HOME SWEET HOME" are often seen in Amish homes. The small round appliquéd rug dated 1969, illustrated in Figure 88, signals the end of the production and popular use of this form.

Figure 86. Appliqued shoe heel sofa rug, attributed to member of Petersheim family, Kinzers, Paradise Township, c. 1950. Woven wool fabric and wool yarn on woven wool foundation, 25.5" x 67". *Collection of the Heritage Center of Lancaster County, given by George Lyster in memory of Kimberly Ann Bupp.*

Figure 87. Appliqued shoe heel "WELCOME" rug, unknown Amish maker working in Lancaster County, c. 1960. Woven wool fabric and wool yarn on cotton foundation, 26" x 37". *Collection of the Heritage Center of Lancaster County, given by George Lyster in memory of Kimberly Ann Bupp.*

Figure 88. Appliqued shoe heel dated "1969" rug, unknown Amish maker working in Lancaster County. Woven wool fabric and wool yarn on woven wool foundation, 22" diameter. *Collection of the Heritage Center of Lancaster County, given by George Lyster in memory of Kimberly Ann Bupp.*

A less common needleworked rug used in Amish homes is the pompon rug . The example pictured in Figures 89 and 90 is typical of Lancaster Amish pompon rugs with shadings of one color yarn tufts arranged in a geometric pattern by the maker Mary F. Beiler Zook of Kinzers. She was the wife of Aaron K. Zook, a well-known Lancaster County Amish artist who produced three-dimensional framed works.[11] This example appears to have been made from a prepared kit using a printed cotton backing, seen in Figure 89. The partial notation on one border reads "---rand Rug No. 9465." This is followed by abbreviations for the shades of yarn to be used. However, none of these colors were actually selected to make this rug. Because they were less durable than hooked rugs and most other handsewn floor coverings, the Amish used them in interior rooms such as a hallway or bathroom. The top surface consists of handmade gathered yarn tufts, or pompons. A graph-like grid of intersecting lines was printed on the cotton foundation and the yarn balls were attached to create a geometric pattern.

Figure 89. Detail of rug shown in Figure 90. *Collection of the Heritage Center of Lancaster County, given by George Lyster in memory of Kimberly Ann Bupp.*

Figure 90. Pompon rug, attributed to Mary F. Beiler (Mrs. Aaron K.) Zook (born 1924), Kinzers, Paradise Township, Lancaster County, c. 1955. Cotton pompons sewn on cotton foundation, 27" x 37". *Collection of the Heritage Center of Lancaster County, given by George Lyster in memory of Kimberly Ann Bupp.*

Another unusual rug type, occasionally made by Amish women, is the cross-stitched needlework form. The example seen in Figure 92 may have been made for a table cover rather than the floor as it is light in weight and would probably not stand up under foot traffic. Unlike the cross-stitched examples created by Church of the Brethren women working in Dauphin County, illustrated in Figures 93 through 100 on pages 77 through 83, this piece is not solidly stitched but relies on the burlap backing as contrast and background for the pattern. The technique closely resembles the much finer cross-stitched patterns executed on fine linen foundation that one finds on Pennsylvania German samplers and decorated hand towels, as seen in Figure 96.

Generally speaking, Amish rugs produced in the Lancaster, Pennsylvania community used materials recycled or left over from family clothing and reflect the color scheme seen in other household textiles. Particularly prior to 1940 wool was the fabric of choice. There were many professional Amish rug hookers who created and used inherited patterns in making rugs for sale within the community and to their English neighbors. Large numbers of similar rugs were also made by Amish women for use within their own homes or to be given to children as dowry items. As a result this close knit community created an easily identifiable body of home made floor coverings.

Figure 91. Detail of cross-stitched rug seen in Figure 92 showing exposed burlap foundation. *Private collection.*

Figure 92. Cross-stitched rug, unknown Amish maker working in Lancaster County, c. 1940. Wool yarn cross-stitched on burlap foundation, cotton backing, 18.5" x 37". *Private collection.*

Dauphin County Cross-stitched Rugs

Another example of a tight knit community of rugmakers were a small group of women, mostly members of the Church of the Brethren, or "Dunkards"[12] living on neighboring farms located in East and West Hanover and Derry Township, and the village of Derry Church, all in Dauphin County. The village of Derry Church was renamed Hershey in1906 in honor of Milton Hershey, the famed chocolate entrepreneur.

The earliest dated example in this group is also the smallest, measuring 20 x 36 inches, and is illustrated in Figure 93. It is signed and dated "Mary Gingrich Derry Church Dauphin County Pa. 1876." Mary (1832-1921) was the daughter of Henry and Lydia Gingrich who owned farms and homes in Annville Township, Lebanon County and later East Hanover and Derry Townships in Dauphin County. She also had a sister Leah. Other signed or initialed examples are: Figure 98, signed "Leah Gingich" and "Kate Lingle;" Figure 99, initialed and dated "KL 1935," attributed to Kate Lingle; Figure 100 initialed "R R" and attributed to Rebecca S. Rauch who later married Moses M. Gingrich (1849-1941), youngest brother of Mary and Leah Gingrich.[13]

A group of rugs made by these women all contain similar yarns used to work the front surface and a light weight burlap that serves as the foundation material. With the exception of one hooked example, illustrated in Figure 97 they are all solidly cross-stitched on this burlap foundation and backed with a light weight colored cotton material. See Figures 94 and 95.

The yarns used are of a two-ply twist, dyed in strong colors that appear to be similar dye lots. The two-ply wool yarns show no evidence of recycling, damage or fading prior to incorporation into the rugs. This would suggest that the makers had access to yarns being used by one of the many woolen mills located in this Dauphin County area in the late 19th century. Very likely these were mill ends and odd lots of materials that were available for little cost.

Unlike most hand made Pennsylvania floor rugs that have a single directional visual orientation, such as a picture to be hung on a wall, these cross-stitched rugs are visually oriented to any direction, similar to traditional homespun tablecloths and wedding handkerchiefs found in Pennsylvania German homes in this region. This 360-degree orientation might suggest that these pieces were intended as table covers, not as floor coverings. Other respected scholars suggest that this design layout may have been influenced by the makers' familiarity with Oriental rugs.[14]

This interesting group of rugs has only recently been studied in detail even though they have been known to collectors of the Pennsylvania German Arts for over 75 years.[15] As additional examples surface there is the likelihood of learning more about these makers and the sources of their materials and patterns.

In more recent decades rug hooking has seen a resurgance in popularity with hookers forming guilds and clubs that meet to share techniques, materials, and social contacts and consume the proliferation of commercial publications available on the craft. In today's world this community is spread even wider through popular websites and chat groups on the Internet. We are no longer in a world where communities of rug makers are limited by geographic boundaries.

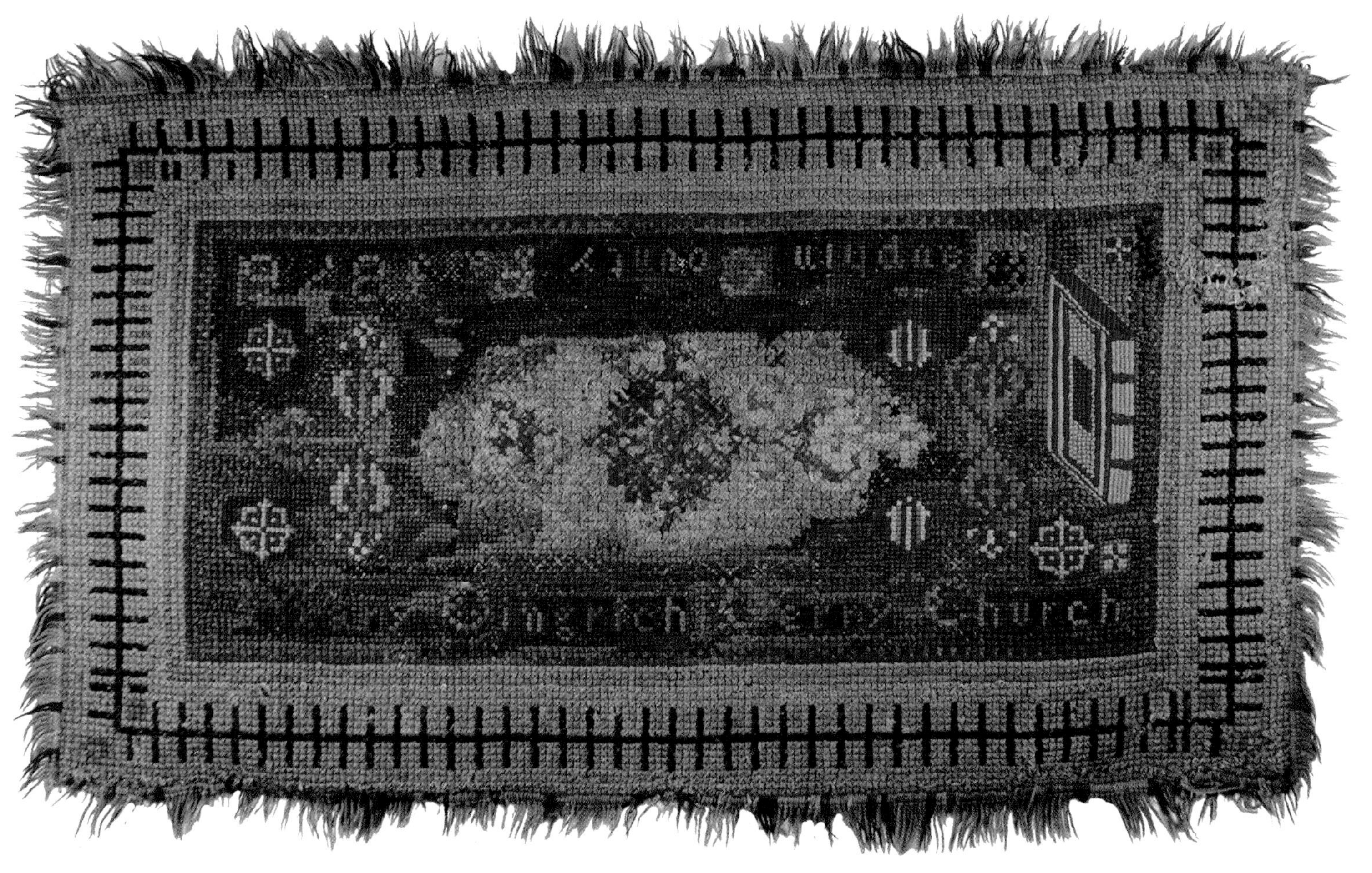

Figure 93. Cross-stitched rug signed "Mary Gingrich Derry Church Dauphin County Pa. 1876." Wool yarn cross-stitched on burlap foundation, twill weave cotton backing, hand made applied yarn fringe, 20" x 36". *Private collection.*

Figure 94. Cross-stitched rug, attributed to an unknown Church of the Brethren member working in Dauphin County c. 1876. Wool yarn cross-stitched on burlap foundation, wool buttonhole stitch edge, woven plain weave plaid cotton back, 36" x 54". *Private collection.*

The earliest dated example uses black and dark brown wool yarns as background and the latest example is worked with a lighter tan wool. All of the needle worked examples use traditional Pennsylvania German cross-stitched motifs most frequently seen on samplers, decorated hand towels, handkerchiefs, and tablecloths. A portion of a decorated linen hand towel with similar motifs is seen in Figure 96. It was made in 1828 by Mary Burkholder (1801-47), a Pennsylvania German Mennonite girl living in Lancaster County.

Figure 95. Detail of rug pictured in Figure 94 showing front, back, and buttonhole stitch edged surfaces. *Private collection.*

Figure 96. Detail of Pennsylvania German motifs worked on decorated hand towel, made by Mary Burkholder (1801-47), Lancaster County, 1828. Cotton and silk thread cross, chain, and overcast stitching on plain weave linen foundation, 60" x 17.5". *Private collection.*

The one known hooked rug of this group, Figure 97, contains fibers identical in weight, color, and twist to all the other cross-stitched rugs of this group except the latest example that is dated 1935 and is lighter in color. The hooked example does not have the cotton backing shared by the other cross-stitched rugs. Being of a heavier weight with no backing and a single visual direction suggests this rug was made to use on the floor. It bears the initials "MH" and was purchased in the 1980s at a house sale of a Hershey family living in the town of Hershey, Pennsylvania.[16] The paired birds and tree motif were commonly used in the 18th and 19th centuries to decorate Pennsylvania German household items and textiles such as coverlets, hand towels, and samplers.

Figure 97. Hooked rug initialed "MH", attributed to member of Hershey family, Derry Church (Hershey) Pennsylvania, c. 1880. Wool yarn on burlap foundation. 24" x 48". *Private collection.*

Figure 98. Cross-stitched rug signed "Leah Gingrich/Kate Lingle," Dauphin County, c. 1876. Wool yarn cross-stitched on burlap foundation, plaid plain weave linen backing, wool yarn buttonhole stitched edge. *Private collection.*

Figure 99. Cross-stitched rug initialed and dated "KL 1935", attributed to Kate Lingle, Dauphin County. Wool yarn cross-stitched on burlap foundation, plain weave checked cotton back, wool yarn buttonhole stitched edge. 35" x 44". *Private collection.*

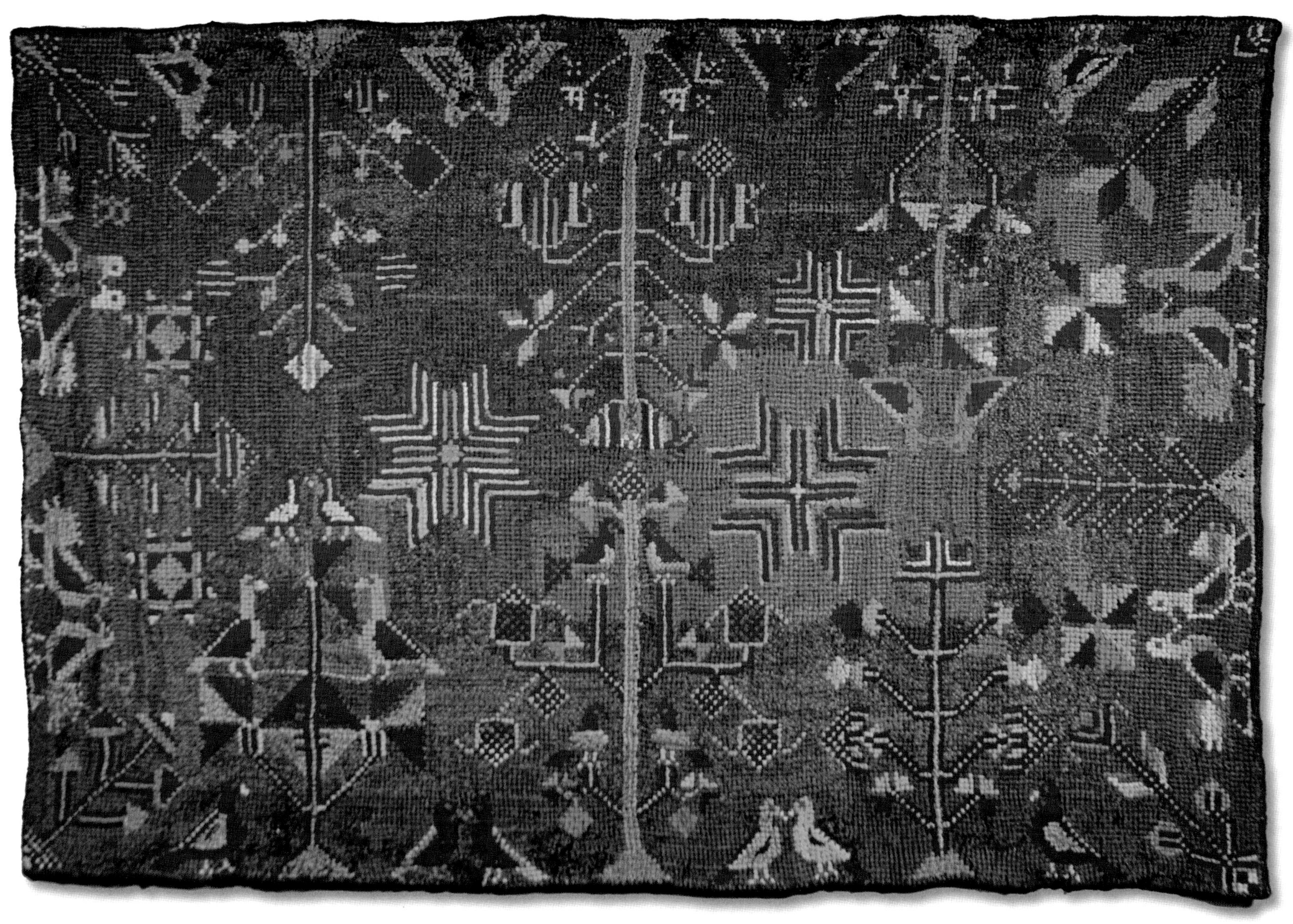

Figure 100. Cross-stitched rug initialed "RR", attributed to Rachel S. Rauch, East Hanover Township, Dauphin County, c. 1876. Wool yarn cross-stitched on burlap foundation, twill weave cotton backing, wool yarn buttonhole stitched edge, 29" x 43". *Collection of Clarke Hess.*

CHAPTER 6

Geometry On The Floor

Many geometric patterns rugs appear to have been made from commercial patterns. The example pictured in Figure 101 is probably such a piece. Using wool yarn hooked on burlap the maker utilized bright colors and a bold geometric pattern similar to what is seen in Lancaster County quilts made in the late 19th and early 20th centuries. This brick-patterned rug was made more recently, probably in the 1940s.

Figure 101. Brick pattern rug, unknown maker working in southeastern Pennsylvania, c. 1940. Wool yarn hooked on burlap foundation, plain weave cotton fabric edge, 33" x 60.5". *Collection of Michael McCue and Michael Rothstein.*

Another geometric pattern that closely resembles the pieced quilt patterns found in southeastern Pennsylvania is illustrated in Figure 102. Similar to a Log Cabin quilt pattern, this example is attributed to Isabelle Zerbey of Schaefferstown, Lebanon County. It features multiple striped borders, also common to quilts of that area.

Figure 102. Block pattern rug, attributed to Isabelle Zerbey, Schaefferstown, Lebanon County, c. 1950. Woven wool strips on burlap foundation, pattern woven wool binding, 21.5" x 31.5". *Collection of Clarke Hess.*

Often it is difficult to categorize a rug into a specific pattern group. The block and floral example shown in Figure 103 certainly could be considered a floral rug, but its basic design structure is geometric. A number of other rugs seen in this study were similar; featuring flowers distributed within an organized geometric grid.

The person thought to have made this well-planned rug was Sue Hummel who lived in Elizabethtown in northern Lancaster County. The rug had been purchased by members of the Greider family as a gift for Martha Greider Herr before her marriage in 1927. A figural rug with a similar history is illustrated in Figure 156 on page 136.

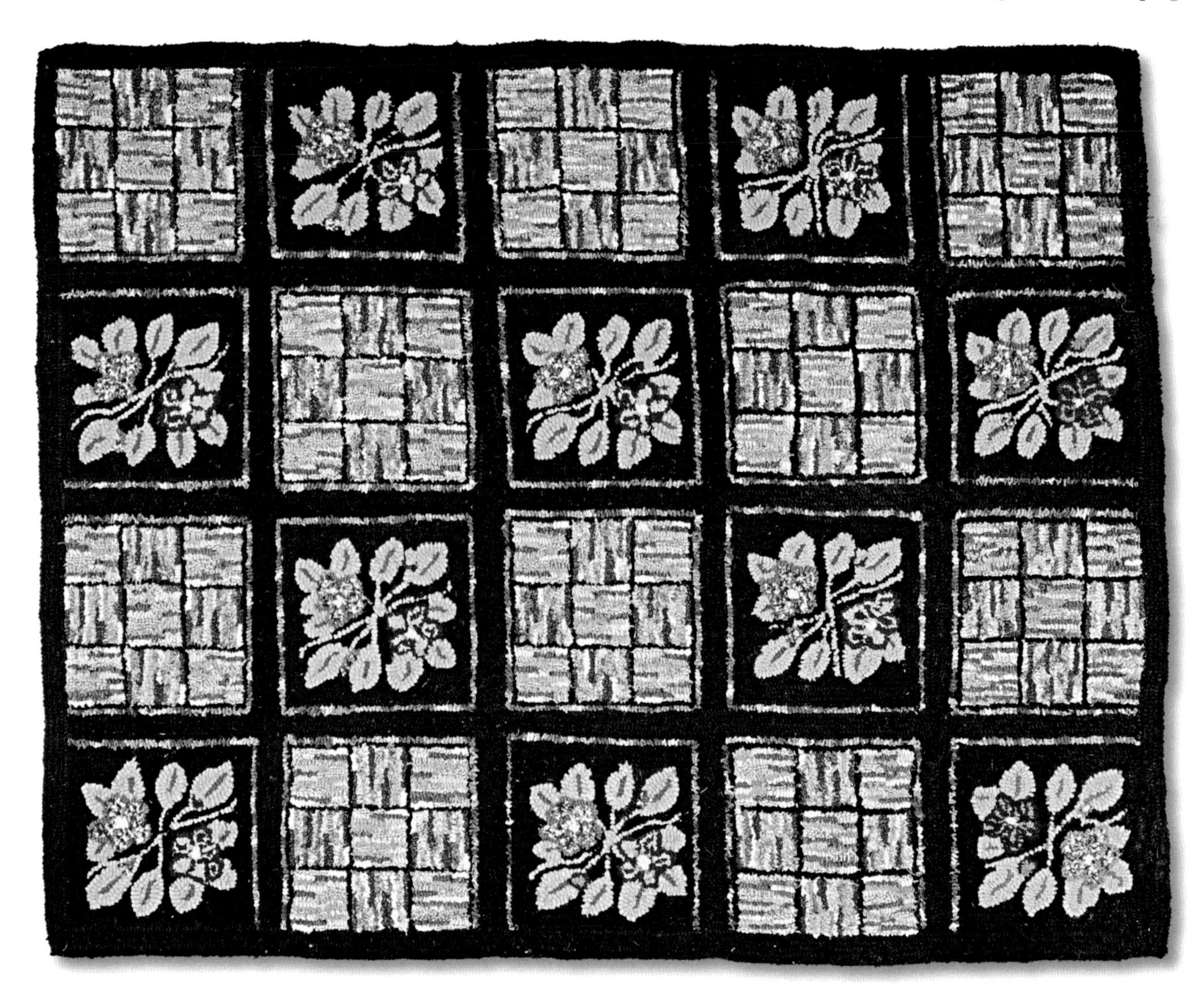

Figure 103. Nine patch block and flower rug attributed to Sue Hummel, Elizabethtown, Lancaster County, c.1925.103oven wool strips on burlap foundation, cotton twill tape binding, 38" x 47". *Private collection.*

A more curvilinear patterned rug is pictured in Figure 104. Likely made in the early 20th century this rug consists of wool and rag strips hooked on burlap and backed with an interesting blue printed cotton material that probably dates from the late 19th century. Figure 105 reveals a closer view of the rug.

Figure 104. Scroll pattern rug, unknown maker working in southeastern Pennsylvania, c. 1915. Woven wool and rag strips on burlap foundation, printed cotton back. 24" x 39.5". *Collection of Nailor Antiques.*

Figure 105. Detail of rug shown in Figure 104 picturing blue printed cotton backing and mixed wool and rag hooking. *Collection of Nailor Antiques.*

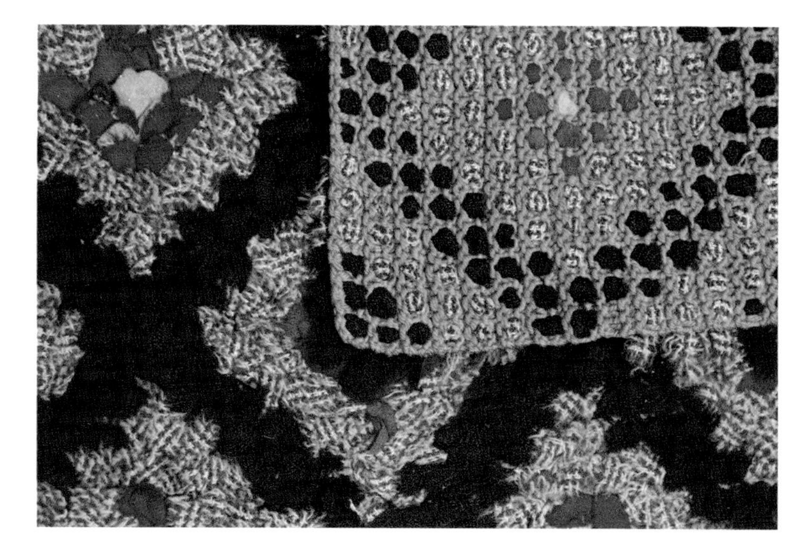

Figure 106. Detail of rug illustrated in Figure 107 highlighting unusual hand knit cotton foundation fabric and clipped top surface of hooked yarns. *Collection of Nailor Antiques.*

The most unusual geometric patterned example was found in a home in Lititz, Lancaster County. This rug, illustrated in Figure 107, was probably an original creation by the maker. As seen in a close-up photograph, Figure 106, showing back and front, the wool strips were hooked into a hand knit cotton foundation and clipped short so no loops are evident on the top surface. This structure is similar to some examples attributed to Shaker makers, but has a solid local provenance.[17]

Because of their seemingly common appearance many other examples of geometric patterned rugs can still be found in use in homes throughout southeastern Pennsylvania. Hopefully their owners understand the importance of these treasures and will preserve them as cherished family heirlooms.

Figure 107. Geometric clipped surface rug, unknown maker, Lititz, Lancaster County, c.1935. Woven wool strips on hand knit cotton foundation, 18" x 30". *Collection of Nailor Antiques.*

CHAPTER 7

Abstract By Design

The rug shown in Figure 108 was found in a Mennonite home in Lancaster County. Although this overall abstract pattern is not unique, most similar published examples are original designs. The rug is constructed of evenly hooked wool strips on a burlap foundation and appears to have been worked by an experienced rugmaker. It also appears to be an original design.

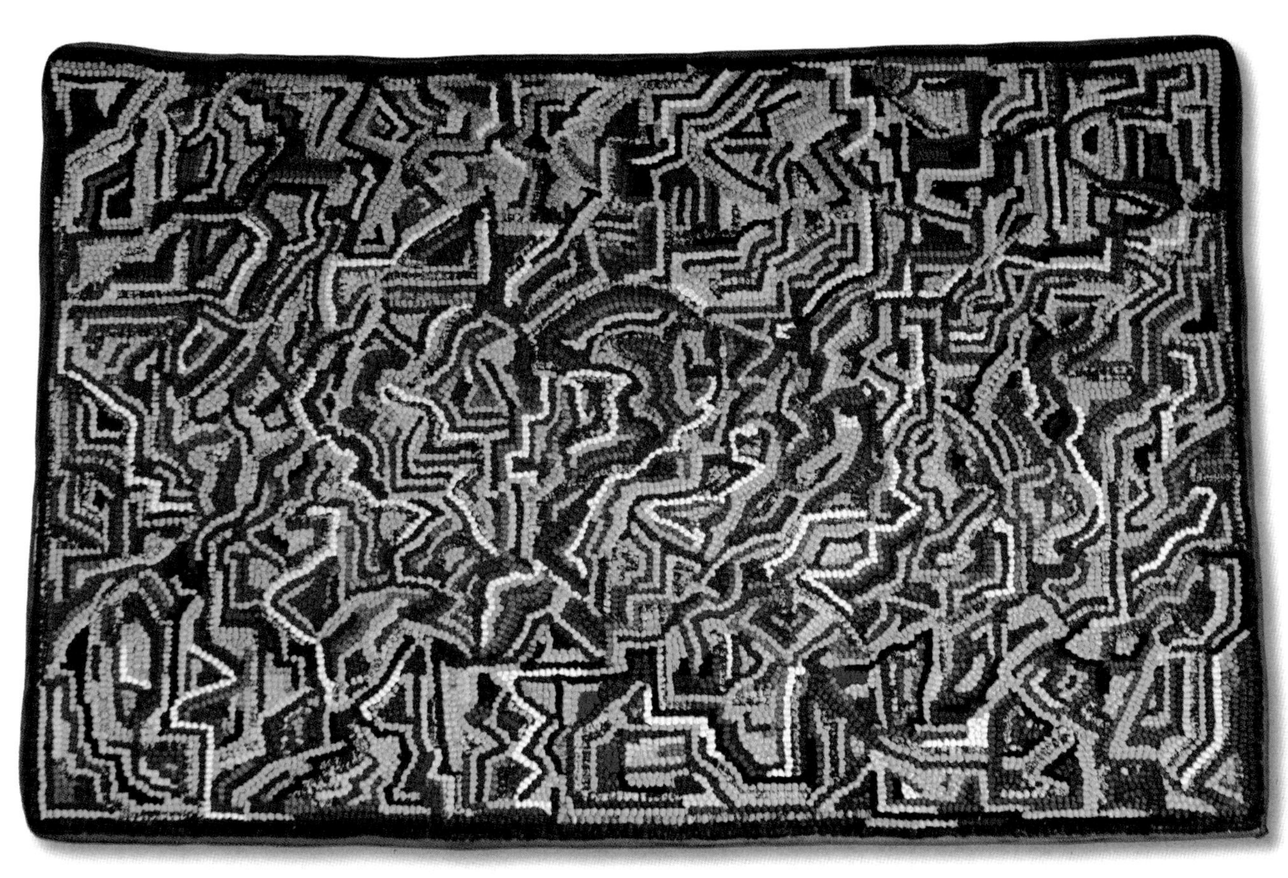

Figure 108. Mosaic rug unknown Mennonite maker, Lancaster County, c. 1935. Woven wool strips on burlap foundation, cotton tape binding, 29.5" x 38.5". *Collection of Nailor Antiques.*

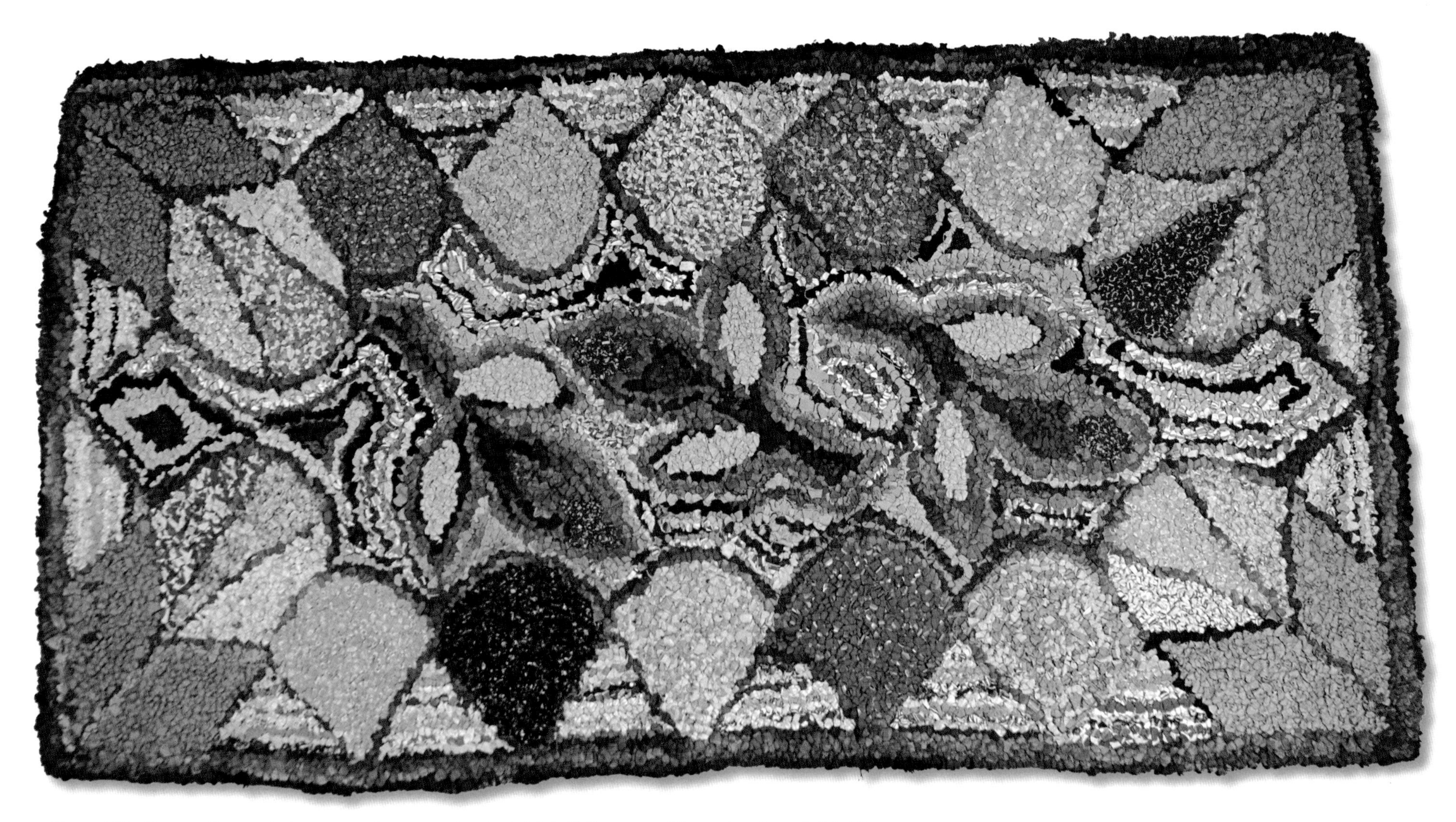

Figure109. Abstract flower design rug, unknown maker in Lehigh Valley area of Pennsylvania, c. 1935. Woven wool and rag strips on burlap foundation, tape binding, 25" x 46.5". *Collection of Kathryn Moyer.*

The two rather abstract fruit and floral rugs, seen in Figures 109 through 112, were found in the Lehigh Valley area of the Commonwealth. They are both similar in size and appear to be made as floor coverings. Hooked from a combination of rag strips on a burlap foundation they share a somewhat organized yet not representational design but do not appear to be made by the same maker. Both have delineated borders and a central focus. The rug seen in Figures 109 and 110 has readily identifiable rosebuds as the central motif. It is hooked from variegated colored fabrics strips coarsely cut and hooked in a random manner. The example in Figures 111 and 112 is made up of finely cut strips with more solid areas of color. One might interpret the objects in the four corners of this rug to be pomegranates.

Figure 110. A corner of the back side of the rug shown in Figure 109. *Collection of Kathryn Moyer.*

Abstract patterned rugs were the least common category of rug documented in the project. Since we lack any maker input concerning these unusual examples, viewers should be free to interpret them in any way they wish.

Figure 111. Abstract fruit design rug, unknown maker, Lehigh Valley area of Pennsylvania, c. 1935. Woven wool and rag strips on burlap foundation, overcast woven wool strip binding, 25" x 46.5". *Collection of Kathryn Moyer.*

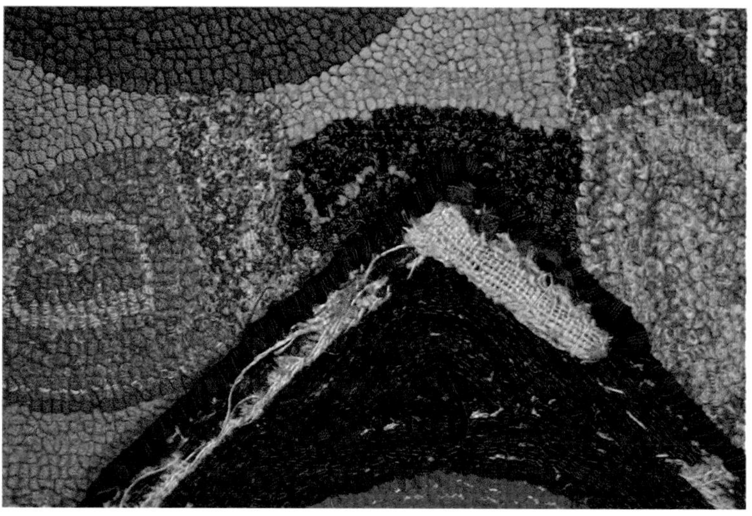

Figure 112. Detail of rug pictured in Figure 111, highlighting overcast woven striped wool strip binding and mixed rag and wool hooking on burlap foundation. *Collection of Kathryn Moyer.*

CHAPTER 8

Botanical Beauties

Probably the most frequently seen hooked rug patterns in Pennsylvania are those depicting flowers, leaves, and fruits.

The oval-shaped rug is a form that adapts well to floral motifs. The example seen in Figure 113 is attributed to Nettie Hess Nolt and made for grandson M. Jack Nolt. Nettie and her husband Harlan, both pictured in Figure 114, lived in Bareville, Upper Leacock Township, Lancaster County.

Family members say she made two rugs for each of her grandchildren. The materials she used for her hooking came from mill ends obtained from the Maytown Manufacturing Company, pictured in Figure 115, owned by her two sons. It appears that this rug was made using or copying a commercial pattern.

Figure 113. Floral pattern oval rug, attributed to Nettie Hess Nolt, Bareville, Lancaster County, c. 1955. Woven rag and nylon mill ends on burlap foundation, 36.5" x 51.5". *Collection of Jack and Ruth Nolt.*

Figure 114. Photograph of Harlan and Nettie Hess Nolt c. 1913. *Collection of Jack and Ruth Nolt.*

Figure 115. Photograph of Maytown Manufacturing Company c. 1955. Mill owned by sons of Harlan and Nettie Nolt and source of mill end fabrics for Nettie's rugs. *Collection of Jack and Ruth Nolt.*

Judging by the photograph seen in Figure 116, Alice Herr Zander (1858-1952) was the maker of many floral and leaf patterned rugs. This picture was taken of Alice sometime in 1950 at the age of 92, the year she was also featured in a local newspaper article.[18] According to the article Zander "...attributes her zest for living to her vital interest in hooked rug making. In 72 years she has made close to 2,000 rugs, varying in sizes, shapes and designs."

The article goes on to say:

> Friends and neighbors contribute their old clothes and "rummage" periodically for wool materials which hook well without raveling.
>
> The older the rags, the easier they are to work with, she claims, because they become soft with age. Her only tools are a pair of scissors and a hook.
>
> Years ago, Mrs. Zander used hooks which she made herself from hickory wood, but she had difficulty with the points breaking off. In recent years she has been using a hook made by her son from an eight-penny nail.
>
> After cutting the rags, Mrs. Zander stencils flowers and other conventionalized designs on the burlap base. She uses no pattern. Hooking constantly, she averages about three rugs in two weeks.
>
> "I don't know what I would do to pass the day if I could not make rugs," Mrs. Zander said.
>
> "I learned when I was first married and have been hooking ever since," she added.

Figure 116. Photograph of Alice Herr Zander, c. 1950, surrounded by her floral patterned rugs. *Collection of Miriam Hershey.*

The rugs seen in Figure 117 and 118 are said to be original designs by Alice who lived in New Providence, Providence Township, Lancaster County. The patterns of these two rugs express an unihibited free form approach to the floral and leaf designs that is also reflected in some of the earlier rugs she made that appear in the photograph with Zander. Like many residents in that area of southern Lancaster County Alice Herr Zander was a direct 7th generation descendant of Hans Herr, father of the first Mennonite family that settled in Lancaster County. Her family believes that these loosely hooked examples were made later in her life, possibly in the 1940s or 50s They also remember Alice using burlap that she had recycled from old feed and grain bags.

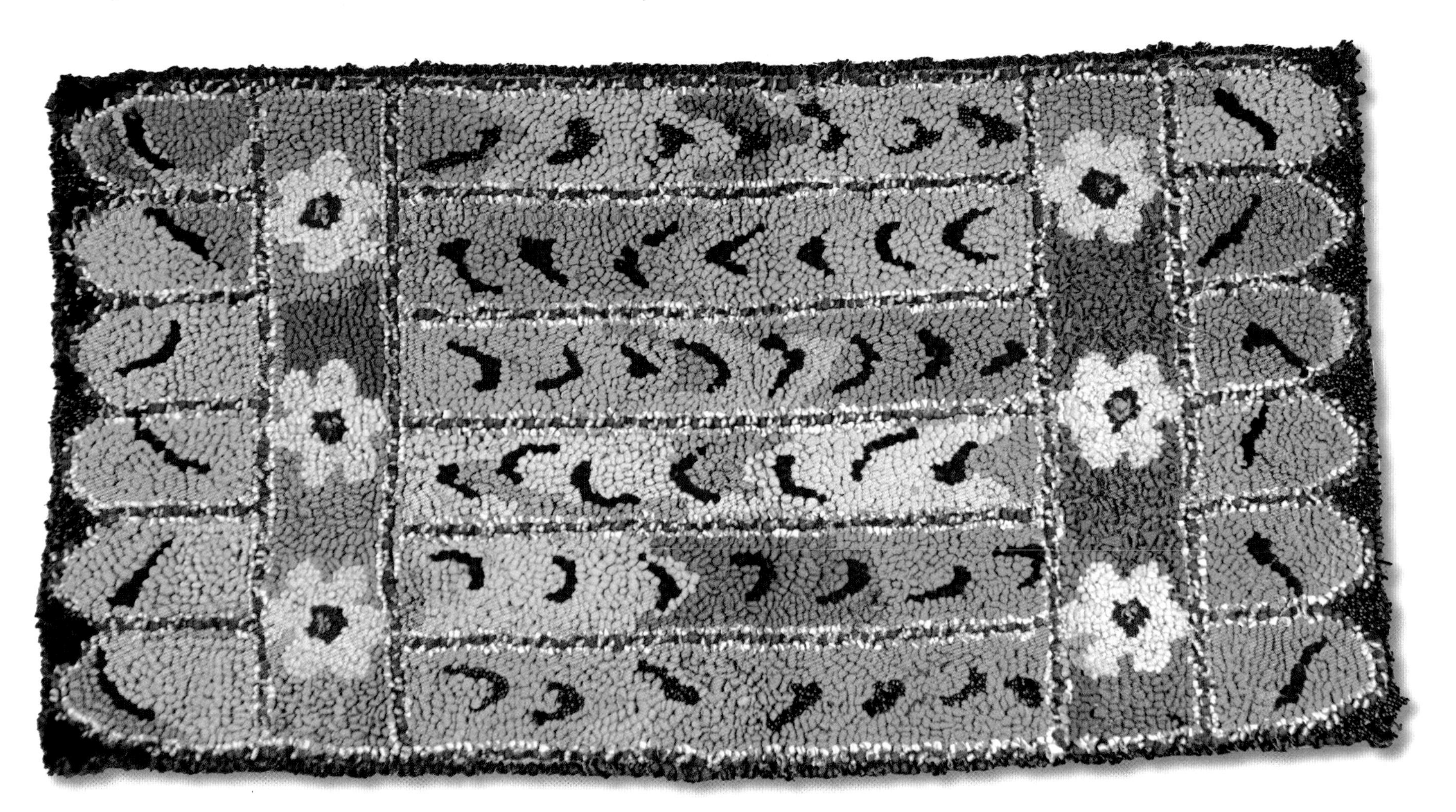

Figure 117. Floral and geometric pattern rug, attributed to Alice Herr Zander, New Providence/Strasburg area, Lancaster County, c. 1950. Woven and knit rag strips on burlap foundation, 19" x 36.5". *Collection of Miriam Hershey.*

Figure 118. Floral and geometric pattern rug, attributed to Alice Herr Zander, New Providence/Strasburg area, Lancaster County, c. 1950. Woven and knit rag strips on burlap foundation, 21" x 36.5". *Collection of Miriam Hershey.*

Two other Lancaster County floral motif rugs are pictured in Figures 119 and 120. Both rugs feature a central basket of flowers and appear to have been made or inspired by similar commercial patterns.

The example seen is Figure 119 was found in Mt. Joy. It is neatly hooked from wool and rag strips using a pleasing variegated "hit or miss" background to offset and complement the bright red flowers and other brown tones used throughout.

The floral basket that appears in Figure 120 is unusual because the maker was a Mennonite retired farmer named Landis R. Heller (1883-1972) who lived in East Lampeter Township. Only one other rug in this survey, pictured on page 152, Figure 172, was known to have been made by a man. Like this example, it also was made from yarn, not cut strips of material.

Figure 119. Flower basket rug, unknown maker, Mt. Joy, Lancaster County, c. 1935. Woven wool and rag on burlap foundation, 26" x 42.5". *Collection of Clarke Hess.*

Figure 120. Flower basket rug, attributed to Mennonite Landis R. Heller (1883-?) retired Mennonite farmer, East Lampeter, Lancaster County, c. 1965. Wool yarn on cotton foundation, 23.5" x 36". *Collection of Clarke Hess.*

The small mat, with a central rose and diamond border, seen in Figure 121, is made of finely cut knitted wool strips evenly hooked in straight rows. The mostly geometric pattern makes this an easier task. The consistency of weight, fabric content, and knitted structure of the hooking material suggests that these fabrics were purchased as mill ends. The size and fine work seem appropriate for service as a table or lamp rug. The use of orange, red and yellow hues are reminiscent of colors found is many Pennsylvania German quilts.

Figure 121. Rose and diamond mat, unknown maker working in southeastern Pennsylvania, c. 1930. Knit wool strips on burlap foundation, 17.75" x 18.5". *Collection of Michael McCue and Michael Rothstein.*

Floral motifs were popular with Amish rug makers and have already been discussed in Chapter 5. The Amish rug pictured in Figure 122 varies slightly from those traditional forms. The design includes a central potted plant surrounded by a narrow inner border. A single blossom just barely breaks through that purple border interrupting its perfect continuity. This unusual variance in the orderliness of Amish rugs makes one wonder how traditional this rugmaker was.

When looking at large groups of rugs as was done in the Heritage Center of Lancaster County Museum's Rug Harvest, it becomes obvious that floral rugs were among the most popular patterns used as floor coverings in early 20th century southeastern Pennsylvania homes. The content of Alice Potter Fordney's inventory of completed rugs and patterns would suggest that handmade floral patterned rugs were in great demand commercially among home decorators, department stores, and antiques dealers selling to wealthy collectors. These patterns appear to have been popular accents in the mansions of the most wealthy as well as the unsophisticated homes of rural women who made their own floor coverings from used clothing remnants.

Figure 122. Flower pot rug, unknown Amish woman working in Lancaster County, c. 1940. Woven wool strips on burlap foundation, cotton flannel edge, 23.5" x 42". *Private collection.*

CHAPTER 9

Pictorial Patterns

Rugs displaying interior views of the home and scenes of the countryside were made throughout America in the early 20th c. But within these categories there are certain patterns that appear indigenous to Southeastern Pennsylvania.

Interior room views often feature a fireside scene, probably influenced by the romanticism of the colonial revival period. New England, the Mid-Atlantic, and Midwest areas each have their own interpretations, but the fireplace scene rugs pictured here are typical of the southeastern Pennsylvania region.

Few hooked rugs are dated but the example, illustrated in Figure 123 on the following page, bears the date 1930 and initials of the Mennonite maker, Minnie Nissley Stehman, the daughter of Reuben Stehman and Anna Wolgemuth Stehman of Mount Joy Township, Lancaster County. Minnie lived in Penn Township, Lancaster County when this rug was made. Known as a prolific rug maker she hooked for sale and for her own use. The rug has a tag sewn on the backing that reads, "fire-place sell $8." Probably because of the effect of the Great Depression, this rug never sold and was passed down to Minnie's daughter Anna Mae.

Although it is likely that Minnie was influenced by other fireplace rug designs, it appears this was her own design. It is larger than most examples with a more elaborate border and interior detail. But the constant images shared with other local fireplace scenes include: the central fireplace containing pots, fire, and clock on the mantel; windows; the presence three oval floor braided rugs; at least one pet; and pictures on the wall.

Figure 123. Fireplace scene rug, signed and dated "MS 1930" made by Minnie Nissley Stehman (1883-1951). Woven wool strips on burlap, 24/5" x 39". *Collection of Clarke Hess.*

The fireplace rug seen in Figure 124 is attributed to Jennie Wolfe Fair of Lincoln, Lancaster County. She and her husband Samuel were owners of the local tavern, now known as the Olde Lincoln House. Family history suggests that Jennie started hooking rugs on her doctor's advice around 1940 and went on to make and sell many rugs. This example also boasts a stone fireplace but without a chimney outline. Generally speaking it is less elaborate in design but still retains the obligatory fireside cat and a special homey wall plaque reading "IN GOD WE TRUST."

Figure 124. Fireplace scene rug, attributed to Jennie Wolfe Fair, Lincoln, Lancaster County, c. 1940. Knitted wool strips and woven rag on burlap foundation, 27" x 50". *Collection of Gail Donahue and Carol A. Maxwell.*

The last fireplace scene, illustrated in Figure 125 was probably also made in the 1940s. It contains some metallic threads used for outlining the curtain and mantel plates, an unusual feature to be seen in rugs. Again the cat appears playing with its ball of yarn. There is no doubt that these scenes are related and probably resulted from exchanges and copying of friends' and neighbors' rug patterns.

Figure 125. Fireplace scene rug, unknown maker, Reinholds, Lancaster County, c. 1945. Woven wool strips and metallic thread on burlap foundation, 24.5" x 39". Collection *of William and Barbara Hazlett.*

Specific views of family homes and farms and idyllic country scenes appear to be popular rug patterns particularly among the rural Pennsylvania German rug makers. Some of these scenes were obviously taken from real life. The imposing rug image of Snavely Mill, located in Lititz, Lancaster County, pictured in Figure 127 is attributed to Lydia Peachy, a Mennonite woman living in the Big Valley area in central Pennsylvania. It was made sometime in the 1940s for a Mennonite friend Nora S. Hershey, who lived in Lititz near the mill. Peachy, using the photograph seen in Figure 126, did an excellent job of retaining the perspective of the original image as she transferred it to the hooked surface of the rug.

Figure 126. Photograph of Snavely Mill near Lititz, Lancaster County, c. 1940. Image of mill sent to maker, Lydia H. Peachy so she could make rug pictured in Figure 127 as gift to her friend Nora S. Hershey who lived near mill. *Private collection.*

Figure 127. Snavely Mill rug, attributed to Lydia H. Peachy (1905-1987), Bellville, Mifflin County, c. 1940. Woven wool strips on burlap foundation, burlap edge, 31" x 50". *Private collection.*

The farm scene rug that appears in Figure 128 also depicts an actual scene. It is believed to have been made by Rebecca Horst Keiffer (1885-1963) as an image of her family home place, Grandview Farm located near Center Church, Bowmansville, Brecknock Township, Lancaster County. The date on the barn, 1907, most likely represents the date the barn was built. The rug itself, which contains great detail, dates from the 1930s.

Probably copied from a period photograph, Kieffer's view features a typical Pennsylvania German barn with overhanging forebay and lower stable doors and windows. Note the detailed barn decoration with name of the farm and date "19Grandview07," and images of draft horses. Visible nearby is the early 19th century family farmhouse. It is common in this productive farming region for the barn to be a great deal larger than the farmhouse.

Figure 128. Grandview Farm rug, attributed to Rebecca Horst Kieffer (1885-1963), c. 1935. Woven wool and rag strips on burlap foundation, 26" x 46.5". *Collection of Clarke Hess.*

The rug seen in Figure 129 presents an idyllic scene, possibly two children walking to school, or perhaps a farmer walking down the path toward home, followed by his obedient bonneted wife. In the foreground, in front of the prim building, wall, and gateway, are a picturesque duck pond and large kettle cooking over the fire. All are nostalgic images that might have graced the floor of a less than picture-perfect home. This rug was probably hooked by the same maker as the following example, seen in Figure 130, containing the image of a covered bridge.

The techniques and fabrics used in the covered bridge rug appear to be the same as those found in the previous house scene. Similar branching tree motifs are also shared. If the maker did not design her own rugs she certainly used the same pattern source. The covered bridge was a common image used to typify the classic folk image of scenic southeastern Pennsylvania in the early part of the 20th century. This rug was probably hooked in the 1940s.

Figure 129. House and pond scene rug, unknown maker (likely same person who made covered bridge scene illustrated in Figure 130) working in Lancaster County, c. 1940. Woven wool strips on burlap foundation, plain weave tape edge, 32" x 53". *Collection of Sam and Kathy McClearen.*

Figure 130. Covered bridge rug, unknown maker (probably same as person who hooked rug shown in 129) working in Lancaster County, c. 1940. Woven wool strips on burlap foundation, plain weave tape edge, 32" x 53". *Collection of Sam and Kathy McClearen.*

Along with covered bridges the image of the Conestoga wagon is closely associated with the farm regions of southeastern Pennsylvania. This romanticized portrayal of 18th and 19th century farmers probably taking their goods to the Philadelphia market, by way of the old turnpike, along with visions of this wagon opening the West to settlers, has been promoted throughout most of the 20th century. Used as logos for businesses, museums, and folk festivals the covered wagon is known world wide as the Conestoga wagon. The name comes from an area in southern Lancaster County that includes the village of Conestoga located in Conestoga Township along the Conestoga River.

The 1950s' rug, seen in Figure 131, is attributed to Edith Harnish Gerhart (1905-1978) who lived in Lititz, Lancaster County. The scene also includes a view of a typical Southeastern Pennsylvania mill with its large mill wheel, located by a stream that provides water power. In this depiction the wagon is being pulled by the traditional six horse team with the driver mounted on the back left horse, often referred to as the wheel horse.

The Gerhart family remembers Edith using recycled old clothing, even though the family could afford to purchase new materials. She kept a rug frame set up in the upstairs hallway or back bedroom of her home where good light was available. Here she was known to have created her own designs, but she may have seen pictures of this popular scene or other rugs that influenced her pattern.

Figure 131. Conestoga wagon rug, attributed to Edith Harnish Gerhart (1905-1978), Lititz, Lancaster County, c. 1950. Woven wool and rag strips on burlap foundation, applied corduroy binding, 28" x 76". *Collection of Roger and Marj Gerhart.*

Another, slightly earlier rug, containing the image of a Conestoga wagon is illustrated in Figure 132. This rendition is drawn by a four horse team, with sets of bells, often associated with the Conestoga wagon, prominently mounted over the withers of the near-sided horses. Accessories such as these bells and the decorated tool box, that can also be seen on the side of this wagon, are sought after as collector's items. This rug, by an unknown Lancaster County maker, appears to be less diagrammatic and possibly an original design.

There were likely many Lancaster County rug makers in the early twentieth century producing rugs containing a Conestoga wagon. One such maker who is said to have designed her own patterns was Katie (Mrs. Joseph I.) Riehl Coblentz (1914-1984), a Mennonite woman living in Christiana, Lancaster County.[19]

Many other interior and outdoor scenes can be found on southeastern Pennsylvania rugs, but the examples shown here were selected because they are representative of the Pennsylvania German culture and not likely to be seen in other areas of the country.

Figure 132. Conestoga wagon rug, unknown maker working in Lancaster County, c. 1945. Woven wool and rag strips on burlap foundation, 26" x 46.5". *Collection of Clarke Hess.*

CHAPTER 10

Figural Floorcoverings

When assessing museum exhibits, private collections, books on decorative arts, and antiques shows and sales one sees a large percentage of hooked and handsewn rugs featuring animal images. This is likely a result of selective filtration. Public collections of household textile furnishings have often been gathered over a period of time by an individual or group looking at the objects as a form of art and not as functional pieces the maker intended to use.

Figural animal rugs, such as dogs, cats, horses, and birds, seem to be most popular among contemporary collectors. But if one has the opportunity to study undisturbed groups of rugs produced for use—multi-generation household estates, the oral family history passed on through descendants of the majority of rug makers interviewed during the Museum's Rug Harvest, and specific collections such as the contents of the estate of rug producer and marketer Alice Potter Fordney, on pages 40 through 55, Figures 42 to 63—these figural forms appear to be less common than floral-patterned rugs.

Rugs featuring horses are frequently seen in the Amish households of Lancaster County where horses are still a part of everyday life for all Amish families. The rug illustrated on page 63, in Figure 78, is a typical example. The horses in this popular design appear in a very diagrammatic form closely following a popular pattern. The Amish rug seenon page 64, in Figure 79, characterizes the horses in a more natural pose, leisurely trotting in a pasture alongside one another.

The Lebanon County rug seen in Figure 133, on the next page, that pictures confrontal horses, is also a popular motif. The pattern used for this rug is a variant of those seen throughout Southeastern Pennsylvania from the late 19th through the 20th centuries. This Lebanon County example is a simplified version with a plain background and only rudimentary tree forms in the foreground. It features the common but unlikely scene of two horses trotting at breakneck speed in a collision path. The wool materials used in this Lebanon County rug are consistent in weight and color shadings, suggesting that the maker had enough of each fabric to plan ahead and not run out of a pattern or background color.

Figure 133. Facing horses rug, unknown maker working in Lebanon County, c. 1940. Woven wool strips and yarn on burlap foundation, machine woven wool and cotton applied fringe, 25.5" x 50". *Collection of Lebanon County Historical Society.*

Another horse rug pictured in Figure 134 features a pair of even more active rearing galloping horses, appearing to be approaching a head-on disaster. They are surrounded by borders containing numerous hearts and pairs of birds arranged in a pleasing well-balanced manner. Although highly decorative and a fine example of folk art, this example appears to be an original pattern made from a wide variety of recycled rag and wool fabrics and could also be classified as "salvage" art.

Figure 134. Rearing horses with birds and hearts rug, unknown maker, Hamburg area, Berks County, c. 1910. woven wool and rag strips on burlap foundation backed with late 19th century cotton fabric, 27.5" x 39.5". *Photograph courtesy of Olde Hope Antiques.*

A pair of less active confrontal horses is seen in Figure 135. They also are hooked from coarser strips of mixed rag and wool materials that vary a great deal in shadings even within the bodies of the horses and color groupings in the border and background. This suggests that the maker also created her work from salvaged fabrics. The handling of these materials adds to the naïveté and charm of the piece.

Figure 135. Facing horses rug, unknown maker working in southeastern Pennsylvania, c. 1920. Woven wool and rag strips on burlap foundation, 22.5" x 40". *Gift of Mr. and Mrs. Irwin Schorsch, collection of the Heritage Center of Lancaster County.*

The lively prancing horse that appears in the rug shown in Figure 136 is also hooked from a variety of wool and rag cloth strips. In this case the variations in fabric colors are used in a more sophisticated manner as shading. The maker also manages to use the color changes to portray activity and motion in the prancing animal. This piece was found in the Oley Valley area of Berks County.

Figure 136. Prancing horse rug, unknown maker, Oley Valley, Berks County, c. 1910. Woven wool and rag strips on burlap foundation, 30" x 37". *Collection of Linda and Dennis Moyer.*

As with the previous example, not all "rug horses" come in pairs or teams. The horse seen in Figure 137 appears to be racing off to the right. The "hit or miss" randomly selected background adds to the motion of the animal. The border, in contrast, consists of heavy solid triangles. This is another example of a combination of coarsely cut recycled wool and rag fabrics that add to the overall interest of the piece.

Figure 137. Running horse rug, unknown maker, southeastern Pennsylvania, c. 1890. Woven wool and rag strips on burlap foundation, 30" x 54". *Collection of Michael McCue and Michael Rothstein.*

The horse, or perhaps mule, represented on the rug shown in Figure 138 is more passive but no less interesting than the previous equine. The creator of this engaging piece manages to give real personality to the figure and adds interest by inserting the bold heart and floral motifs in the corners. This small floor covering no doubt gave great pleasure to its maker, as it does to all who view it today.

Figure 138. Standing horse with hearts rug, unknown maker working in Franklin County, c. 1890. Woven wool and rag strips on burlap foundation, 28" x 56". *Photograph courtesy of Olde Hope Antiques.*

The rug depicting a single horse rug facing to the left, illustrated in Figure 139, uses matching wool and rag strips rather than the hit or miss style in the previous example. Although not as fluid in its design, its naïve character suggests that the pattern originated with its maker. The rug was purchased from a Mennonite family living in the Blue Ball area of Lancaster County.

Figure 139. Standing horse rug, unknown maker, Earl or East Earl Township, Lancaster County, c. 1915. Woven wool and rag strips on burlap foundation, 26.5" x 41.5". *Collection of Nan and Jim Tshudy.*

Dogs were also a subject popular with Pennsylvania rug makers. The rug pictured in Figure 140, containing two black dogs face-to-face, comes from the same Mennonite household as the previous horse rug. Note the similar hooking style and fabrics utilized in both pieces. Again, this simple design probably originated with the maker.

Figure 140. Facing dogs rug, unknown maker, Earl or East Earl Township, Lancaster County, c. 1915. Woven wool and rag strips on burlap foundation, 21" x 39". *Collection of Nan and Jim Tshudy.*

The sad-eyed Basset Hound pictured in Figure 141 also appears to be an original design, probably a dear family pet drawn from life by an unidentified maker working in Hampton, Adams County. Originally a French breed, the Basset Hound was introduced to America in 1885, and had gained popularity in America by the early 20th century when this rug was made. The hooking materials are all wool and well matched suggesting that this rug was carefully planned and not just a result of haphazard construction. The surrounding rose designs may have been adapted from other rugs the maker had seen, but this appears to have been a single work made to honor a special family member.

Figure 141. Bassett Hound rug, unknown maker, Hampton, Adams County, c. 1930. Woven wool strips on burlap foundation, 20" x 45". *Collection of Dr. Sharron Nelson.*

A bright bold addition to the floor of any home would be this red-toed panting black dog from York County, illustrated in Figure 142. In a seeming haphazard, but delightful manner, the areas surrounding thc pooch are filled with leaves, stars or flowers, fill-in blocks, and a big blue bird. Judging by the bright colors and fabric selection this example was probably made in the late19th century.

Figure 142. Dog rug, unknown maker, southeastern Pennsylvania, c. 1890. Woven rag strips on burlap foundation, 27.5" x 38". *Collection of Anne Bedics and Thomas Kort.*

Perhaps the most stylized dog rug design is seen in Figure 143. Tightly and evenly woven of similar weight wool fabric strips, this intense canine gaze captures the viewer's attention. The unknown Lancaster County maker used a variety of background fabrics that were well chosen so as not to detract from the central image and clearly defined flower and border design.

Figure 143. Dog rug, unknown maker, southeastern Pennsylvania, c. 1925. Woven wool strips on burlap foundation, 36" c 49". *Photograph courtesy of Olde Hope Antiques.*

Cats cannot be ignored as inspiration for rug designs. There were many commercial designs available featuring cats, but the following examples illustrate how women incorporated the feline figure into their creations. The rug pictured in Figure 144 is unquestionably an original design likely copied from a real life companion. If one looks closely, twelve tan birds can be seen surrounding the cat on all borders. Because there has been some fading of the flock, they are barely discernable except for their red and purple highlights. The black cat, accentuated by four black stars, appears as the central figure, aloof, as only cats can be.

Figure 144. Cat rug, unknown maker, southeastern Pennsylvania, c. 1900. Woven wool and rag strips on burlap foundation, 33" x 45". *Collection of Anne Bedics and Thomas Kort.*

Although not the only animal appearing in the rug shown in Figure 145, the central orange cat predominates. The maker, a member of the Lehman family living in Deodate, Dauphin County, probably created this original design in the early 20th century. It was made from a variety of clothing materials, some suffering more wear than others from daily use. But the naive design combines the large orange cat, small prancing horse, and paired roosting birds in a delightful manner.

Figure 145. Cat rug, member of Anna Mary Lehman family, Deodate, Dauphin County, c. 1920. Woven wool and rag strips on burlap foundation, 22" x 39". *Private collection.*

The brown cat, pictured in Figure 146, on a rug within a rug, appears comfortably nestled among the roses. Other interesting aspects of this example are the applied cotton dotted fabric eyes, applied hand-braided stripping used to make the 1901, and the small kitten perched on its back. The creator of this original design also made the 1897 example illustrated in Figure 147.

This earlier example, dated 1899, depicts a decidedly happy sheep surrounded by flowers similar to those used in the previous 1901 cat rug. The borders are also well defined and executed. These rugs were found in northern Lancaster County.

Figure 146. Cat rug dated 1901, unknown maker (likely the same as Figure 147), northern Lancaster County. Woven wool, rag, and wool yarn on burlap foundation, plain weave cotton backing, applied machine woven wool fringe on side edges, 26" x 39". *Private collection.*

Figure 147. Sheep rug dated 1897, unknown maker (see Figure 146), northern Lancaster County. Woven wool, rag, and wool yarn on burlap foundation, plain weave cotton backing, applied machine woven wool fringe on side edges, 26" x 40". *Private collection.*

The sheep rug seen in Figure 148, probably made in the 1930s, is from Lebanon County. It was found together with the floral rug pictured in Figure 149. They are likely the work of the same unidentified maker. Both rugs appear to have been made from identical yarns and burlap foundation, backed with small print cotton dress materials, and sewn together in a similar fashion. The hooking was done in even rows and is consistent throughout. It is likely they were done using a commercial pattern. There is a similarity in the rose design used in the outer free-flowing border of the sheep rug and the roses inset in the block border of the more geometric piece.

Figure 148. Sheep rug, unknown maker, Lebanon County, (see Figure 149) c. 1930. Wool yarn on burlap foundation, plain weave printed cotton backing, 28" x 49". *Lebanon County Historical Society.*

Figure 149. Floral and geometric pattern rug, unknown maker, Lebanon County (likely same maker as Figure 148), c. 1930. Wool yarn on burlap foundation, plain weave printed cotton backing, 19.5" x 38". *Lebanon County Historical Society.*

Birds were also a popular subject for rug makers. The white dove rug, seen in Figure 150, is the earliest dated Pennsylvania rug seen in this study. It was found in Lancaster County. 1887 appears hooked in light colored fabric in the upper right corner. But a closer look reveals another darker date located just below the bird's breast. The use of multiple colors of recycled wool fabrics for the background just adds interest to this original design.

Figure 150. White bird rug dated 1887, unknown maker, Lancaster County. Woven wool and rag strips on burlap foundation, 30.5" x 41". *Photograph courtesy of Olde Hope Antiques.*

Another dated example pictured in Figure 151 features a pair of large eagles in the top corners, well balanced with paired red birds, smaller cats, and tiny dogs below. Large flowers, a variegated background, and central 1908 date add to the vitality of this piece. As with many original patterns designed by Pennsylvania makers, this hooker was not concerned about appropriate perspective when she hooked this delightful rug.

Figure 151. Eagle rug dated 1908, unknown maker, southeastern Pennsylvania. Woven wool and rag strips and wool yarn on burlap foundation, hand crocheted cotton applied edge, 30.5"x 48". *Private collection.*

Perhaps the boldest and most colorful example of the bird designs documented is the bird tree rug, illustrated in Figure 152. It was found in the Gettysburg area of Adams County. The unknown maker's creation is enhanced by her choice of bright solid red for the birds' bodies against a well planned blue strip background. All this is set off with the multicolored feather border and black surround.

Figure 152. Birds and tree rug, unknown maker, Gettysburg, Pennsylvania, c. 1920. Woven wool and rag strips on burlap foundation, dimensions unknown. *Photograph courtesy of Olde Hope Antiques.*

A rug containing a single bird, illustrated in Figure 153, appears to have been made sometime around 1900. In this imaginative example, the small bird is perched on a rather thin floating rose branch, holding another huge rose "twig" in its beak. The unknown maker, who worked in Erwinna, Bucks County, also added interest by filling each corner with a trifid motif.

Figure 153. Bird and rose rug, unknown maker, Erwinna, Bucks County, c. 1920. Woven wool and rag strips on burlap foundation, 21" x 33". *Photograph courtesy of Olde Hope Antiques.*

Many rug makers pride themselves with selecting high quality wool fabrics to insure their creation will wear well and provide warmth and comfort to a room. The house where this rug, pictured in Figure 154, was found was small, poorly maintained, and located in a marginal farming area. So it may have been by necessity that this maker used pieces of flimsy worn cotton material that would truly be classified as rags. Her efforts to make an attractive rug however proved successful. These chickens no doubt provided a cheerful addition to this home.

Figure 154. Chicken rug, unknown maker, Mastersonville, Lancaster County, c. 1930. .Woven rag strips on burlap foundation, 29" x 46". *Private collection.*

Rabbits are not commonly seen as images on Pennsylvania rugs. This example pictured in Figure 155 would bring a smile to anyone's face. It was purchased from a Mennonite family living in the Manheim area of Rapho Township in northern Lancaster County. Using recycled clothing and household materials did not inhibit the maker's sense of humor. Wouldn't it be interesting to have known this individual? The variegated fabric strips used as background seem to add the charm and motion of these "dancing bunnies."

Other examples of rugs featuring animal motifs are featured in the discussion of rugs attributed to Magdalena Briner/Eby, on pages 148 to 150, figures 168 through 170.

Figure 155. Rabbit rug, unknown maker, Manheim area, Rapho Township, Lancaster County, c. 1940. Rag on burlap foundation, 18.75" x 30.5". *Collection of Sam and Kathy McClearen.*

One could consider the colorful oval rug seen in Figure 156 in the category of birds. But this squawking goose appears to be chased by a bonneted Bo-Peep type character. The effect is one suggesting a Mother Goose story and was likely a pattern with some name pertaining to a storybook character.

The rug is attributed to Sue Hummel a resident of Elizabethtown, Lancaster County. The geometric and floral patterned rug pictured in Figure 103 on page 86 is also thought to have been made by Hummel. She made it from yarn and recycled fabrics for members of the Greider family who gave it to their daughter Martha Greider Herr before her marriage to Maurice Herr in 1927. Herr always kept it in an upstairs guest room that was seldom used.

Figure 156. Girl and goose rug, attributed to Sue Hummel, Elizabethtown, Lancaster County, c. 1925. Woven wool and rag strips on burlap foundation, 27" x 48". *Private collection.*

Another interpretation of a human figure on a rug is the Dutch girl motif hooked into the small mat illustrated in Figure 157. This too appears to be a commercial pattern, probably made in the 1960s. It was purchased at a public auction of the possessions of three unmarried Mennonite sisters and likely provided an exotic focal point in a traditional Lancaster County Mennonite household.

From this small sampling one can begin to appreciate the variety of figural rugs made in southeastern Pennsylvania. It is likely that museums and contemporary collectors will continue to place a high value on this category of rugs. As a result they will continue to be discovered, collected, and cherished.

Figure 157. Dutch girl rug, attributed to three unmarried Mennonite women, Leola, Lancaster County, c. 1965. Woven wool strips on burlap foundation, 18.5" x 24.5". *Collection of William and Barbara Hazlett.*

CHAPTER 11

Special Rugs, Special People

Many of the rugs found in this survey did not appear to have personal connections with family members and special events within family life, and this may be another reason they were not valued for more than their functional use.

Figure 158. Photograph of Helen Morgart Brubaker, whose rug is seen in Figure 159, c. 1944, the same period in which the rug was made. *Collection of Florence Brubaker.*

Fortunately there are a variety of engaging and poignant tales associated with some of the documented examples that otherwise might not be considered unusual. The rug shown in Figure 159, simulating an Oriental carpet, was made by Helen Morgart Brubaker (1896-1968) of Bird in Hand, Lancaster Co. Helen started working on the rug, made with a latch hook kit, in the 1940s to keep herself busy while her sons were away fighting in World War II. Her photograph, taken at about that time, is seen in Figure 158. When she finished the rug she cried. Her sons returned from overseas and she never hooked a rug again. Her descendents treasure this piece.

Figure 159. Oriental design latch hook rug made by Helen Morgart Brubaker, Bird-in-Hand, Lancaster County, c. 1944. Wool yarn latch hooked on burlap foundation stamped with "Persia," buttonhole stitched edge, 35" x 58". *Collection of Florence Brubaker.*

The rug pictured in Figure 160 was hooked by Ida Roher Mellinger (1866-1944), a Mennonite woman living in Soudersburg, Lancaster County. According to her family she made a good many rugs in her lifetime. This particular piece was inherited by her daughter Edith Ann Mellinger Metzler who, late in life after her mother had passed away, remarried at the age of 77. Because of the association of this rug with her deceased mother, Edith chose to stand on it, in a home marriage ceremony, with her husband-to-be, Ira Herr. This tree of life pattern rug now has been passed on to the next generation and has special meaning to Edith's daughter.

Figure 160. Tree of life rug, attributed to Ida Rohrer Mellinger, (1866-1944) Mennonite woman living in Soudersburg, Lancaster County, woven wool strips on burlap foundation, 38" x 65". *Collection of Mrs. Charles H. Leaman.*

When Mennonite Anna Charles' daughter Carolyn was married to Robert Clayton Wenger, owner of C. P. Wenger and Sons feed mill in Ephrata, Carolyn asked her mother to make a special rug. She gave her mother, an experienced rug hooker, a burlap feed bag with the company logo printed on its face. Anna, using yarns in colors similar to the printing on the bag, created a rug in the image of the company's product for her son-in-law. Figure 161 pictures the whole rug. Refer to Figure 12 on page 16 for a detailed view of the woolen yarns used in making this unusual piece.

It was common practice for rural women to take used feed or grain bags apart and recycle them into totally different forms to serve as decorative and functional floor coverings. But it is unlikely there are many other rugs created in the image of a feed bag such as this one that Anna Charles created.

Figure 161. Wenger feed bag rug, attributed to Anna Denlinger Landis Charles, Lancaster, Pennsylvania, c. 1979. Wool yarn on burlap foundation, plain weave cotton/blend fabric, 23" x 39". *Collection of Robert and Carolyn Wenger.*

Figure 162. Photograph of Elizabeth (Lizzie) Berger Engle (1852-1952), maker of rug pictured in Figure 163, and her husband George Engle, c. 1900. *Collection of Evelyn Schreiber.*

Lizzie Berger Engle (1852-1952), whose image appears beside her husband, George, in the photograph seen in Figure 162, is another interesting Lancaster County resident who hooked many rugs in her long life. Her Swiss ancestors became members of the River Brethren Church after coming to America in 1754. She grew up on a farm in Washington Boro, southern Lancaster County, that was part of the Underground Railroad prior to, and during, the Civil War. Escaping slaves were hid, slept, and were fed in the family barn before traveling further north. Following the war, Lizzie watched Lincoln's funeral train as it returned from Illinois.

Late in life, when she hooked the rug seen in Figure 163, Lizzie Berger Engel was living in the village of East Petersburg, located in East Hempfield Township. Using recycled clothing material she made it using the commercial pattern # 4243A produced by the Hooked Rug Foundation.

Figure 163. Geometric rug from commercial pattern marked "#4243 Hooked Rug Foundation," attributed to Elizabeth (Lizzie) Berger Engle (1852-1952), East Petersburg, Lancaster County, c. 1940. Woven wool and rag strips on burlap foundation, 26" x 42". *Collection of Evelyn Schreiber.*

After marrying George Engle, the couple lived in the Marietta/Maytown tollgate house in northwestern Lancaster County and collected 5 cents from every traveler going on the toll road to the town of Marietta. It is said by family members, seen surrounding her in the photograph shown in Figure 164, that she kept her many rugs in a pile in her living room.

Figure 164. Photograph of Lizzie Berger Engle surrounded by her family in her later years, c. 1930. *Collection of Evelyn Schreiber.*

Another rug maker, well known in her community of Manheim, Pennsylvania was Minnie Shaffner Missimer (1879-1964). She acted as the town historian as well as being an active rug hooker. One of Minnie Missimer's rugs is illustrated in Figure 165. Her technique of using sturdy well-matched woolen yarn and fabric strips is repeated in this large multi-animal rug as well as in her other rendition of the Steigel office. She was obviously an accomplished rugmaker.

Figure 165. Animal rug attributed to Minnie Shaffner Missimer (1879-1964), Manheim, Lancaster County, c. 1940. Woven wool strips and wool yarn on burlap foundation, 46" x 77.5". *Private collection.*

Minnie was living right on the town square, where as a child she would have seen the building depicted on the rug illustrated in Figure 167. The building, destroyed in 1910, had been the office of "Baron" Henry William Stiegel, the colorful iron master, glassmaker, and founder of Manheim. (The Germanic rendition of Steigel's name was Heinrich Wilhelm Stiegel, but Missimer puts in her rug Henry Wilhelm Steigel, a combination of old country and English versions.) Minnie made at least two rugs depicting this building, taking her pattern from a postcard scene pictured in Figure 166. The publisher of this card was Henry F. Ruhl, a druggist and printer in town. Minnie was a good friend of Ruhl's wife and the pair spent many hours together hooking rugs.[20]

Figure 166. Post card "Office of Stiegel, Founder of Manheim, Pa.," published by H. F. Ruhl, Druggist, c. 1910.

Figure 167. "Office.Of.Baron.Henry.Wilhelm.Stiegel" rug, attributed to Minnie Shaffner Missimer (1879-1964), Manheim, Lancaster County, c. 1940. Woven wool strips and wool yarn on burlap foundation, 30" x 52". *Private collection.*

The rugs attributed to Magdalena (spelled various ways in historical records) Briner/Eby (1832- 1915), of Perry County, have become icons of American folk art since they first appeared in noted collections, exhibits, and catalogs in the mid-20th century. Several have been described and reproduced by modern rug makers.[21] Although none are signed or dated, family history suggests they were made in the latter part of the 19th c. and early 20th centuries and can be identified by their "absence of a border, solid, dominant animal forms, rainbow like corner motifs, and a haloing effect around the animal forms."[22]

Figure 168. Eagle with two birds rug attributed to Magdelena Briner/Eby (1832- 1915), Perry County, c. 1890. Woven wool and rag strips on burlap foundation, 30" x 42.5". *Collection of Michael McCue and Michael Rothstein.*

One notices, in the examples illustrated in Figures 168 through 170, these properties: the bold juxtaposition of animals and sometimes flowers, not necessarily in scale and often a contrasting "hit or miss" random color selection of background material. The wool and rag strips are also relatively course and unevenly worked throughout the rug. The combined effect is that of excitement, motion, and primitive appeal.

One of Magdalena's great-granddaughters remembers "walking on the rugs and beating the dust out of them on the clothesline."[23] The family also believes that Magdalena was the only one in the family to have made the surviving rugs that were used throughout the house. They were then sold to an antiques dealer from Carlisle in 1965. Although her rugs bring large sums on today's market, Briner/Eby, like the previous makers mentioned in this chapter, probably made them primarily for family use.

Figure 169. Domestic zoo rug attributed to Magdelena Briner/Eby (1832- 1915), Perry County, c. 1890. Woven wool and rag strips on burlap foundation, 24" x 70". *Photograph courtesy of Olde Hope Antiques.*

Figure 170. Confrontal birds and horses rug attributed to Magdelena Briner/Eby (1832- 1915), Perry County, c. 1890. Woven wool and rag strips on burlap foundation, 51.5" x 46". *Photograph courtesy of Olde Hope Antiques.*

Most of the previous makers have been women, but the creator of the example illustrated in Figure 171, Wilmer S. Moyer (1907-2002), was a resident of Pennsburg, Montgomery County. As a young soldier in WW II, he was seriously wounded and spent time in 1945 in a veteran's hospital in Cambridge, Ohio. As part of his therapy Wilmer was taught to hook rugs. He created an example resembling Bugs Bunny, seen in Figure 172 on page 152, and another similar piece that resembled Porky Pig. Fortunately his family preserved his rugs, hooking materials, and the photograph of Wilmer wearing his Veteran's Aministration hospital garb. Wilmer's rugs appear to be made from a pattern, probably provided by the hospital along with all the rug materials.

It is important that these, and many similar unrecorded "rug yarns," be preserved by families, collectors, and museums. Special people do make special rugs!

Figure 171. Photograph of Wilmer S. Moyer c. 1945 taken while he was recouperating at a Veteran's Administration hospital in Cambridge, Ohio. He made the rug seen in Figure 172 as therapy during treatment of war injuries. *Collection of Linda and Dennis Moyerfor*

Figure 172. "Bugs Bunny" type rug attributed to Wilmer S. Moyer (1907-2002), Pennsburg, Montgomery County, c. 1945. Cotton yarn on burlap foundation, cotton twill tape edge, 30" x 23". *Collection of Linda and Dennis Moyer.*

CHAPTER 12

Conclusion

It would be hard to categorize the rug design seen in Figure 173 on page 154, so it is fitting to have it serve as a conclusion to this discussion of Pennsylvania rugs.

The family of the maker, Anna Hostetter Wolgemuth (1898-1982), believes this was her original design and was made about 1960. Anna was born in Rapho Township, Lancaster County, the daughter and wife of farmers and members of the Brethren in Christ Church. She only began making rugs around 1945 when she moved to the town of Mt. Joy to take care of her father-in-law.

The design of her rug is a map of the Commonwealth of Pennsylvania with each county represented by a block of color with rivers shown in lines of blue. Within each county is a red dot indicating the county seat. In the dark red county of Lancaster there is also a white dot for Anna's hometown, Mt. Joy. The flower in the upper right corner is believed by the family to be Mountain Laurel, the official state flower.

Family members have many fond memories of Wolgemuth and her rug hooking activities. She worked at one end of her dining room next to the window where she had a home made rug frame set up. Beside her chair she kept a bag or basket with coats, trousers, and other heavy materials. From here she would pull out what she wanted and cut it by hand. Some of the fabrics came from a dress factory about a mile away.

She sewed extensively making dresses that were all alike for the cousins and grandchildren. Wolgemuth was known for being creative and, according to the family, made things from anything she could get her hands on. She made a variety of pincushions and collected large juice cans, put them together, and covered them with fabric to create small hassocks.

In the middle of her attic there was a cedar closet in which Anna kept her rugs. When the grandchildren came to visit they were allowed to go up there to see the rugs and at the age of twelve each child was permitted to choose a rug. Today those grown grandchildren treasure the rugs they were given as twelve-year-olds.[24]

Anna Hostetter Wolgemuth's rug represents only one rug and one story among the many documented during this Rug Harvest project supported by the Heritage Center Museum of Lancaster County and all the hard working volunteers who made it happen. There are still many undiscovered rug treasures rescued from the floors of the past that need to be documented for future generations. It is the hope of this author that other groups and organizations in the Commonwealth of Pennsylvania will continue with this exciting work.

Figure 173. Counties of Pennsylvania Map rug, attributed to Anna Hostetter Wolgemuth (1898-1982), Rapho Township, Lancaster County, c. 1960. Woven wool and rag strips on burlap foundation, plain weave striped cotton edge, 27" x 44". *Collection of Ruth E. Heisey.*

Endnotes

Chapter 2. From the Eye Of A Needle

1 This rug has been known to the collecting community since the first half of the 20th century and appears in: Lichten, Frances. *Folk Art of Rural Pennsylvania*. New York: Charles Scribner's Sons, 1946, p.188, and in Hornung, Clarence P., *Treasury of American Design: A Pictorial Survey of Popular Folk Arts Based upon Watercolor Renderings in the Index of American Design at the National Gallery of Art.* New York: Harry N. Abrams, Inc. 1976, vol.II, p. 538.

2 This rug is illustrated in: Newman, Ronnie. *Light from the Past: Early American Rugs from the Collection of Ronnie Newman.* Ridgewood, NJ, 2004, p 31.

Chapter 4. The Business of Rugmaking

3 These papers and other mentioned pictures, letters, and notes may be found in the Archives & Special Collections, Franklin & Marshall College, Lancaster Pennsylvania, MS44 Muench Family Papers, Series LXVI, Box 17, folder 4, and Box 18, folder 14. Other miscellaneous papers are also in the collections of the Heritage Center Museum of Lancaster County.

4 Research done by Gerry G. Heusken Jr., for the Heritage Center Museum of Lancaster County, Pa. July, 2004.

5 The majority of rugs, patterns and other printed materials pertaining to Alice Potter Fordney's rug making activities are in the Sarah Muench (Fordney's niece) estate collections at the Heritage Center Museum of Lancaster County.

6 Hess, Clarke. *Mennonite Arts.* Atglen, Pennsylvania, 2002, p. 121.

7 The interview was conducted on October 21, 2004 at Willow Valley Retirement communities with Sarah McIlvaine Muench by Wendell Zercher, curator of collections of the Heritage Center Museum of Lancaster County, Pennsylvania.

Chapter 5. Rug Making Within The Community

8 Herr, Patricia T., in Kraybill, Donald B., *et al., A Quiet Spirit: Amish Quilts from the Collection of Cindy Tietze & Stuart* Hodash (Los Angeles: UCHA Fowler Museum, 1996), pp. 52-53.This study provides an analysis of Lancaster Amish home textile production from Amish women's diary sources.

9 Personal communication with Thomas L. Wentzel, researcher and collector, November 5, 1997.

10 McCauley, Daniel and Kathryn, *Decorative Arts of the Amish of Lancaster County* (Intercourse, Pa.: Good Books, 1988), p. 74.

11 Herr, Patricia T., *Amish Arts of Lancaster County*, (Atglen, PA: Schiffer Publishing Ltd., 1998), p. 37.

12 The slang term "Dunkard" or "Dunkar" refers to the baptismal practice of total immersion or "dunking" practiced by members of the Church of the Brethren.

13 The author thanks Clarke Hess for his detailed research on these rug makers he has so kindly shared.

14 Personal communication with Dr. Irwin Richman, professor emeritus of American studies and history, Penn State Harrisburg and Peter Seibert, president of the Heritage Center Museum of Lancaster County. It is the author's opinion that these isolated Church of the Brethren women would have had little chance for exposure to Oriental carpets or their images.

15 Examples of similar rugs can be found in some of the collections amassed by early collectors Henry Frances du Pont at Winterthur Museum in Delaware and Mrs. J. Inslee Blair and Bernice Chrysler Garbisch at the Metropolitan Museum of Art in New York City. For more information on one of the Metropolitan Museum of Art's examples see *Folk Art of Rural Pennsylvania*, (New York: Charles Scribner's Sons, 1946) p. 189.

16 Personal communication between the collector, at the time of purchase of the rug and the dealer Chris Machmer, Hamburg, Pa.

Chapter 6. Geomety On The Floor

17 Personal communication by author with Sam McClearan, antiques dealer who purchased this rug at a house sale in Lititz, Lancaster, Pa.

Chapter 8. Botanical Beauties

18 Excerpts from the Lancaster, Pennsylvania Sunday News, July 16, 1950.

Chapter 9. Pictorial Patterns

19 Information provided to author by Tom Martin, Interpreter, Landis Valley Museum, Lancaster, Pennsylvania, February, 2008.

Chapter 11. Special Rugs, Special People

20 Information obtained from Anna Enck, previous owner of the rug and a former neighbor of the rug maker, September 17, 2002.

21 Lawrence, Evelyn, 2004, "Antique Primitive Rugs: a Search for the Rugs of Magdalena Briner," *Rug Hooking*, Volume XV, Number 4, January/February 2004.

22 Ibid., This quote by Joel Kopp was taken from the previously sited article. Kopp is the coauthor, with his wife Kate of the book *American Hooked and Sewn Rugs: Folk Art Underfoot* (New York: E.P. Dutton). The Kopps, antiques dealers, have handled a number of Briner/Eby rugs over the years. This author is indebted to Evelyn Lawrence for her enthusiastic and helpful assistance on obtaining documented information on Magdelena Briner/Eby, her family and her rug making. Most of the information put forth in this section is directly from the article listed above.

23 *Ibid.*, p. 28.

Chapter 12. Conclusion

24 Information gathered from the family of the rug maker during the Heritage Center Museum of Lancaster County Rug Harvest project.

Bibliography

Garvin, Beatrice B. and Charles F. Hummel. *The Pennsylvania Germans: A Celebration of Their Arts 1683-1850*. Philadelphia: Philadelphia Museum of Art, 1982.

Garvin, Beatrice B. and Charles F. Hummel. *Pennsylvania German Art 1683-1850*. Chicago and London: The University of Chicago Press, 1984.

Herr, Patricia T. *Amish Arts of Lancaster County*. Atglen, Pennsylvania: Schiffer Publishing, Ltd., 1998.

Hersh, Tandy and Charles. *Samplers of the Pennsylvania Germans*. Birdsboro, Pennsylvania: The Pennsylvania German Society, 1991.

Hess, Clarke. *Mennonite Arts*. Atglen, Pennsylvania: Schiffer Publishing, Ltd., 2002.

Lichten, Frances. *Folk Art of Rural Pennsylvania*. New York: Charles Scribner's Sons, 1946.

McCauley, Daniel and Kathryn. *Decorative Arts of the Amish of Lancaster County*. Intercourse, Pennsylvania: Good Books, 1988.

Kopp, Joel and Kate. *Hooked Rugs in the Folk Art Tradition*. New York: Museum of American Folk Art, 1974.

Kopp, Joel and Kate. *American Hooked and Sewn Rugs*. New York: E. P. Dutton Inc., 1975, revised edition 1985.

Schiffer, Margaret. *Historical Needlework of Pennsylvania*. New York: Charles Scribner's Sons, 1968.

Von Rosenstiel, Helene. *American Rugs and Carpets*. New York: William Morrow and Co., Inc., 1978.

Weissman, Judith Reiter and Wendy Lavitt. *Labors of Love*. New York: Alfred A. Knopf, 1987.

Index

rags to rugs
PENNSYLVANIA
Hooked & Handsewn